GHOST STATIONS™ 4

by

Bruce Barrymore Halpenny

L'AQUILA

Based on the original **GHOST STATIONS**™ Series (Copyright © 1986)

This New Edition - first published August 2008

British Library Cataloguing in Publication Data
Halpenny, Bruce Barrymore
1. Great Britain. Royal Air Force. Aerodromes. Ghosts.
2. Paranormal. Mysteries. Supernatural

ISBN-10: 1-871448-13-1 ISBN-13: 978-1-871448-13-9

L'AQUILA is an imprint of the **ANZIO Group**

Published by:

ANZIO Group
Greetwell Place
2 Limekiln Way
Greetwell Road
LINCOLN
Lincolnshire, England
LN2 4US

www.anzio.co.uk

CONTENTS

GHOST STATIONS™ Acknowledgements

My very special thanks to all who have helped me with the books in the **Ghost Stations™** Series … those who have talked freely about their ghostly encounters - some for the first time - others who have enriched and filled out old stories in my files. Many, many thanks to all those who have loaned me material and photographs and those who so kindly gave me material and photographs to use as I wished. A special mention to Peter Tory of the Daily Express and the Daily Mirror who prompted me to use material collected over the years when researching for my books **Action Stations 2** Military Airfields of Lincolnshire and the East Midlands; **Action Stations 4** Military Airfields of Yorkshire; and, **Action Stations 8** Military Airfields of Greater London**,** and write the ghost/mystery book which, with demand from the public for more, became eight books in the **Ghost Stations™** Series:

John Ainsworth; Allan Allchurch; Mr F.W.E. 'Rik' Appleyard; Richard Allen; Wing Commander H. R. Allen, DFC; Wing Commander David Annand; Mrs. Armstrong (née Bevan); Mr M.J. Arnold; Flight Lieutenant Thomas J. Attrill; Mr R. Austin; Mr P. Avis;

Lord Balfour of Inchrye, PC, MC; Robert A. Bell; Paul Booth; Air Vice-Marshal H. Bird-Wilson, CBE, DSO, DFC, AFC; Mr Ken Billingham; Mrs Ann Binnie; Bob Blunden; Neville Bowles; Mr. J. Brice; Jack Broadhurst; Robert Anthony Brunsdon; Steve Bond; Mrs Joan Brown; Miss Ruth Baker; Mr P. Bennet; Mrs Bowyer; Louise M. Brazier; Mr B. Brennan; Bob Bryan; Mark Bryan; Mr Bob Ballard; Nicholas Bell; Neville Bower; Flight Lieutenant John Brown; Mr J. R. Bushby; Bundesarchiv, Germany;

Mr D. W. S. Chapman; Mrs June Constable; Mr Bill Corfield; Mr Allan Cram; Peter Crowson; Mr Duncan Currie; Squadron Leader Tony Cunnane; Edward 'Herb' Currotte; Mr John McCaughrean; Courtenay; Mrs Vera Chapple; Norman Carless; Mr A. J. Charlton; Squadron Leader John Cole, MBE,CC; Miss Denise Marie Curran; Mrs Beryl Christiansen, USA; R. Coleman; D. A. Cross; Stuart Chapman; Jim Chatterton;

Mr R. C. Daniels; Mr Dennis Davis; Squadron Leader Len Devonshire; Clifford G. Dray; Mr R. Downs; Mr W. Drummond; Dorothy Darwood; Paul Dixon; Mrs Elma Drewry; Wing Commander John H. Dyer; Harry Douse; Ron Day; J. Diamantakos for the Glenn Miller photographs, which were taken by his brother; Betty Dalmond; Mr R. C. Davies; Dennis Davis; David Drew; Squadron Leader Neville Duke, DSO, OBE, DFC; Douglas Durkin; William Deiches - writer and speaker on before Christ History - for permission to quote from the article 'Of Men and Angels'; J.C.Dening; Herr Helmut Dreher, Germany;

Mr. E. A. Easters; J. V. Evans; Mrs Audrey Elcombe; Charles Ekberg; Mrs G. Ettidge; Mark Elliott; Thomas England;

Mrs Alice Farmer; Mr F. Fawke; Mr Bernard Feasey; Squadron Leader Brian Fern; Mr J. L. Fletcher; Robin Fletcher; Syd Frogley; Terrance O'Flynn; Ted Foster; Rosemary Ford; Debbie Francis; Mick Fisher; Captain Laura J. Feldman, The Military Airlift Command, Scott Air Force Base;

Geoff Gardiner; Miss Renee Glynn; Mrs J. Greaves; Mr C. R. Green; Alex Gibson; Colin and Melita Gibson; Peter Giles; Graeme and Janice Garnham; Ralph Gilbert; Stan Galloway; Dr Alan Gauld, Dept. of Psychology, University of Nottingham; Duncan Gray; Mrs Winifred K. Grant; Robert Gray; Mrs Jill Grayson; Janet Gibson; Mrs Joan Goult;

Gareth Hanson; Alan D. Harridence; Mr Derek A. C. Harrison; Mr R. Hawkins; W. Hayes; Mrs Peggy Hayles; Mrs Sheila Heple; Eric Hilton Hewitt; Mr Ian Hogg; Mrs Molly Una Hollis; Stan Holtham; Ex-RAF Sergeant Bernard D. Hughes; Mr E. J. Humphries; Mr Peter Hyde; Bernard Halford; Andrew Hall; Charles Humphrey; Lee Hatfield; Trooper Darryl Hewitt and Carol Hewitt; Geoffrey Hall; Peter Hindley; Mrs Jean Horrocks; Brian Hunter, Rhodesia; Jefrey S. Halik; Mrs Eileen Hodgkins; Heinz von Hahn, Geneve; Werner Hoffmann, Germany; Peter Giles Hull;

Brenda Jackson; Brenda Jenkinson; Mrs R. Jones; Mr E.W. Joyce; Major Robert Keith Jones; Colonel de Jong, Dutch Ministry of Defence; Mr Jack Jones; Ray Jackson; Harry Jury; Alan Jones; Ken Jones; Taffy Jones; Mr & Mrs Jackson;

Mr D. G. Kilvington; Mr G. Kimber; Ian King; Gordon Kinsey; Mr Michael Kelham, MA, Headmaster St. Hugh's School, Woodhall Spa, Lincolnshire; Squadron Leader Ken Kenton; Desmond Keen; Mr J. Keward; Miss Kerry-Leigh Parish,Yeovil;

Mr B. G. Leigh; Ron Lines; Philip Levick; Stephen Lowdon; Gamekeeper Phil Longden; John Langford; Stephen Lewis; Leicester County Council;

Mr Edward (Ted) Marcham; Mrs L.B. McKelvey; Mrs W. Meeson, Wilfred Mills, Mr R.J. Minett; Mrs O. Morton; Neil Mayne; Ministry of Defence, London; Godfrey Mangion, Malta; Mr E.T. Manby; Mrs Carol Marshall; Martin-Baker Aircraft Co. Ltd; Mrs Moor; Wing Commander Martin; Bob McPhie, Founder The Dodo Bird Club, Canada;

Lorimer Dennis O'Driscoll; Mrs Molly O'Loughlin White; Pete O'Brien;

Mrs Dorothy Pickard; Mr Jock Pepper; Mr Norman Pepper; Miss Prudence Pepper; Mrs C. Petre; Archie R. Pratt; Tom Perrott, Chairman of the Ghost Club, London; Bill Perry; David Peel; Harry Pain; Squadron Leader Colin Pomeroy; Captain R. N. Phillips; David Pearson; Peter Phillips; Charles Plumb;

Captain Barry Radley; Adrian Railton; George Rance; Mr Laurence F. Round; Mrs C.A. Russell; Ernie Reynolds; Squadron Leader Derek Rothery; William Reeves; John (Jack) Riley; Adrian Railton; Mr Raynforth; Mrs Reedman; David Rimmer, Chairman, Clwyd Aviation Group; Mr F.A.C. Roper;

Mrs Joyce Schofield; Mr S. Scott; Mr Chas Selway; Mr V. Simons; Mr W.E. Simpson; Cliff Sims; Norman W.T. Skinner; Mr Gordon Slater; Brian Stafford; Mrs V.Summers; Walt Scott; Carl Schulte, Lausanne; James Silver; Derek Smith; Flying Officer Brian Stephenson VR; Edward Stott; Francis A. Smith; Harry Smith; Miss Margaret Sawyer; Jack Smith;Dave Sutton; Dick Sharphouse; M. Sarson; Werner Schmidt, Germany; Frau Schmidt, Frankfurt-on-Main; Sue Smithson, South Africa; Sheila Staves, Australia;

Mrs Mollie E. Tilley; Mary Tock; Frank Thomas, Western Australia; Jim and Molly Thompson; Les Timms; Mrs Sylvia Tucker; John Turner; Lance Tebbutt; Jan Thorpe; Flying Officer Nicky Tilmouth, WRAF; John W. Tilmouth;

Steven Upton;

Alan Waddington; John Roy Walsh; Mr Paddy Ward; Mr R.F. Warren; Flight Lieutenant John Wears; Mrs Shirley G. Westrup; Harry Willmott; Mike Whalley, Editor, Morecambe Visitor; Mr R. Wilkie; Mr E.W. Winkless; Julia Wolfe-Harlow; Mr Bill Wood; Peter Wright; Keith Wardell; Miss J.A.Wilkinson; Mrs Cella

Winstanley; Geoff Whitworth; Denise Williams; Brandon White; William E. Whitehead; Gordon West; Keith Walker; Wilbur Wright;

Jill Yates; Bill and Barbara Young;

I am indebted to the editors of: Air Cadet Journal; Air Force Magazine; Croydon Advertiser Group of Newspapers (G. G. Collard); Daily Mirror - Peter Tory's Diary; Evening Star, Ipswich; Gravesend & Dartford Reporter; Grimsby Evening Telegraph; Lincolnshire Echo; Lincolnshire Standard; Metal Box News - R & D Division Metal Box plc; News of the World (David Gordois); Nottingham Evening Post (Martin Stevenson); Romford Recorder (R. J. Mills); Scottish Daily Recorder & Sunday Mail; Sunday Express (James Kinlay); Sunday Mercury - Birmingham (Peter Mitchell); The Press, Christchurch, New Zealand; Yorkshire Post; Aeroplane Monthly; Airforce Magazine - Canada; Birmingham Mercury; Dodo Club, Station C, Victoria, Canada; Stadtarchive Heilbronn; Die Spiegel; Haller Tagblatt; Flypast Magazine; South Somerset Advertiser; Western Gazette; Western Mail & Echo, for permission to publish the photograph of the haunted restaurant; for their very generous help with request letters, article and permission to quote from published stories. My sincere apologies if I have somewhere quoted from an article or work without acknowledgement, also for photographs. Please contact if one has slipped through my heavy workload.

My special thanks to: Leon Thompson, USA; Neville Franklin - Control Column; Duncan Blair; Mrs Betty Hockey; Ken Border for his help with some of the research; Robin J. Brooks for West Malling photographs; Denny Densham for the articles and for the ORIGINAL tape recordings of the Bircham Newton aerodrome haunting, the ORIGINAL tape-recordings of the Bircham Newton update and of the nights investigation at North Weald aerodrome, and for the ORIGINAL tape-recordings of the investigation at Borley Church, the most haunted church in the world, and, to use as I wish with all the ORIGINAL recordings; Dottore Mario Mignella, Pescara, Italy;

Charlie Chester, Sunday Soapbox Programme; Alex Dickson, Radio Clyde; Keith Skues - Yorkshire Radio Network, Radios Hallam, Viking and Pennine - and Classic Gold Radio; Dennis McCarthy at BBC Radio Nottingham; Hans Plantz for translations; Dave Benfield who sorted out the Glenn Miller photographs; Ted Evans for his military reminiscences and valued help; Mrs Hannah Hunt for the many poems, including 'Breakfast' and 'The long Farewell' with permission to publish as I wish;

David P. Sandeman, Chairman of The House of Sandeman for permission to reproduce the 'Sandeman Don'; my racing friend Harry Coulby; Walter Laidlaw, Scotland; last but not least, my military friend in Germany, Hermann Laage for great camaraderie. Hermann worked hard on some of the later German stories and some of Hermann's stories have photographic proof, which give you food for thought. Let me close with a section from one of Hermann's reports:
"Appropriately enough I am writing you this report at midnight and the bats are bumping against my window. At nightfall the bats start coming out of crevasses or cracks in the hill opposite my house. They live in a sealed tunnel that harboured an underground arms factory of the former NSU Works - the NSU Kettenkrad etc. Now millions of these little Draculas must live there."

The material for all the books in the **Ghost Stations™** Series came from decades of researching and writing about military aviation. Over the years literally thousands of people have contacted me and assisted me and to everyone … Thank you.

INTRODUCTION

My previous books in the first Ghost Stations™ Series brought forth many kind and welcome letters. Mrs Jean Horrocks from Leicester who wrote to say:

"I wonder if my own experiences around the old American airbase at Bruntingthorpe, near Leicester would count for anything. Over the years we have gone out there on a nice summer afternoon, just to enjoy the peace and quiet of the countryside, and invariably as we sit, I hear on the wind, the voices of what I can only think of as young American airmen.

"It really is uncanny, but although I have told friends about it, up to now I have not met anyone else who has heard them. Could it be the Spirits of young men killed in the war, who somehow have come back to a place that despite the dangerous lives they led, have been happy there? It is just a thought."

Mrs Jean Horrocks is not on her own. I have received hundreds of letters saying just that; and many of their stories are published in my Ghost Stations™ books ... the old airfields have an eerie kind of pull; but one that you cannot ignore.

Robert Gray from West Yorkshire wrote to say:

"I simply feel compelled to write to you with an experience that I had while visiting Thorpe Abbotts Airfield in September 1990.

"I had looked over the museum and control tower and as it was a warm sunny day; decided to do some filming of the old taxiways, hardstand and runway. I stopped off at the bunker for a look around, and as I came out I felt a strong presence of someone watching me. I did not see anything, nor did I hear anything, not even any birds. I didn't sense an evil presence; just a slightly sad feeling came over me and the strong sense of someone, or something … watching me.

"It could have been my imagination. I was trying to imagine the sound of B-17s warming up their engines and rolling out to the runway; and what life was generally like on a wartime airfield. But then again, I had had the same thoughts on the other 18 or so airfields that we had visited, on the previous few days; and I had felt nothing at the other stations and they included

Lavenham and Lakenheath, where through your books I have learned of other happenings.

"Now I like to keep an open mind about these things, I am not a firm believer in ghosts simply because I have never seen one … but what I felt that day was eerie."

Robert Gray asked me to point out and make very clear that he was not a publicity seeker, nor had he anything to gain from telling me his story. The old wartime airfields affect people in many ways.

Now all is silent... the runway at North Witham in Lincolnshire. From this very runway the Pathfinder paratroops took-off and set the D-Day invasion in motion … not a sign anywhere to mention this historic even … just the ghosts and sadness.

Balado Bridge a lone building on the once busy Domestic Site. An eerie sadness prevails.

The control tower at Skipton-on-Swale that once pulsed life is now derelict and forlorn. Only the ghost squadrons are now airborne from this once busy bomber airfield.

Neglected and forgotten … the old Nissen Huts that were the Officer Mess on the WAAF *site at East Moor in Yorkshire. The once joyful laughter long since gone … now only memories*

Now all is silent for the crew locker drying rooms at RAF *Winthorpe. They slowly crumble away, no more lies to continue with … just memories, which are tinged with sadness.*

I get hundreds of letters asking to see the old wartime buildings; for many who do visit the old airfields find them gone. So at your leisure, enjoy the 7 lovely pictures that I show on pages 11, 13, 14 15 & 16. These are priceless. The picture on page 11 shows Canadian fighter pilots having a break in Lincolnshire.

I take this opportunity to thank all who write to me; and trust that you will understand it is impossible to reply to all letters. I explain more in the book Ghost Stations™ The Story.

To you all … Cheers,

Bruce Barrymore Halpenny
Roma
Italia

YOU AND I

LET US WALK TOGETHER
You and I,
French, Celt, Saxon and Scot
To the river, the river ours
Yours and mine.

Let us watch, together
You and I,
French, Celt, Saxon and Scot
The ruffled waters, the water ours.
Yours and mine.

Let us together, crew up again,
You and I,
French, Celt, Saxon and Scot
And fly' the silver knitted skies we once made ours.
Yours and mine.

Let us, together, hand in hand
You and I
French, Celt, Saxon and Scot,
Walk towards GOD, a God of ours
Yours and mine.

Let us, together
You and I,
French, Celt, Saxon and Scot,
Forget quarrels, that are not ours,
Nor yours, nor mine.

For some day, together, very still…
You and I
French, Celt, Saxon and Scot,
Will lie in this land, this land of ours.
Yours very yours, my very mine!

Edward 'Herb' Currotte

ECHOES

This poem was specially composed for Ghost Stations™ by my good friend, John Walsh and it sums up very well the feelings of the old wartime airfields … gone … but many earthbound Spirits remain …

ECHOES

There are sounds out there if you listen;
Sad voices from the past,
On the brooding silence of any 'drome when
The purpling night falls fast.
Walk soft passed the crumbling Nissens, are
There whispers on the air?
Does ghost meet ghost in the brief twilight,
Are pale phantoms murmuring there?
Lost spirits of the Commonwealth; Empire and
Allied kin,
Are they out of sight in the fading light
Each night as the dusk draws in?
Stroll passed the gaunt dark hangars, is that
The reek of engine oil,
Do the shades of long dead riggers work on
In their endless toil?
Walk on the windswept runways where once the
Lancs sought flight,
Is the haunting song of the Merlin strong; a
Pulse through the long sad night?
Traverse the long stilled firing butts where
No more the Brownings bark,
Would you dare the ghosts of yesteryear; come
The threat of the looming dark?

THE GHOSTS OF MARTLESHAM HEATH

In 1974 Smith Sample Cases Company moved to a new purpose built building, on the Martlesham Heath Industrial Estate, from their old RAF building that was on the old Martlesham Heath airfield, near Ipswich.

Martlesham Heath housed the Americans during the Second World War. It is an old site, which was used during the First World War, its role being with experimental aircraft.

And, at the outbreak of the Second World War it housed the Aircraft and Armament Experimental Establishment. The airfield became Station 369 in 1943 and in October of that year, the 356th Fighter Group moved in with their P-47 Thunderbolts. The Americans moved out at the end of 1945 and the airfield reverted to the RAF. It remained open after the war and housed a variety of units. It finally closed in 1963.

Deserted and left to fade into history; many strange and eerie stories began to be told about the old airfield. Was the airfield haunted? The answer to that is yes, and it is easy to understand why. Many people have claimed unnerving experiences on the old wartime airfield.

For no logical reason, light aircraft in the vicinity of the old airfield have crashed; and at least three fell under the spell of Martlesham Heath, the pull of the old airfield had them in its supernatural power … and down they came.

The old building that Smith Sample Cases vacated was taken over by Dobie and Partners, a firm of constructional engineers.

A few weeks after their move, Francis Smith, the founder of Smith Sample Cases, met the manager from Dobie and Partners at a trade function. Francis Smith takes up the story: "The first thing he said to me was - 'Mr. Smith you did not tell me that when I moved to your building that I had inherited a ghost' - to which I replied that I was quite unaware that there was one. I asked him if he would describe the ghost, and in which area it was seen, and that I would contact the foreman who was working in the area.

"On returning to my firm I spoke to the carpentry shop foreman, Jimmie Mann and enquired of him if he had ever seen a ghost in his workshop area to which he replied, 'Oh yes a few times when he had been working overtime on his own.' I asked him to describe the ghost and he said it was an airman with a pack on his back which he took to be a parachute, which was the same description as that given to me by the manager of Dobie & Partners.

"I also asked my employee Jimmie Mann, why he had not mentioned these occurrences, and he said: 'I would not dare to as the rest of the staff would take the Mickey out of me.'

"I was very impressed, as I had exactly the same description from each person, and I had no previous knowledge whatever of this occurrence."

MY PROTECTOR

At 0444 hours on Thursday 8th June, 1995, American Air Force pilot, Captain Scott O'Grady, was plucked out of the Bosnia War Zone, and he greeted his rescuers with an amazing statement: "My Guardian Angel kept me alive."

The family of Captain Scott O'Grady, 29, shown briefly on television with a stubby beard as he alighted from the rescue helicopter on to the USS Kearsarge, rejoiced at his rescue.

"We are grateful and so thankful," said Mary Lou Scardapane, Captain O'Grady's mother, outside her home in Seattle, Washington.

Little did she know that it was O'Grady's Guardian Angel she had to be grateful to; for Captain O'Grady believes a Guardian Angel was looking after him. He said he went through a deeply moving experience during his six days in hiding after he was shot down.

"At moments of greatest danger, I could sense that the angel was by my side," revealed Scott to one of the crack U.S. Marines that rescued him.

Over the next few days the Top Gun's incredible story of Faith, Courage and, his Guardian Angel unfolded; so let us go back to the beginning, in order to understand just what took place, during those six days of hide and seek in Serb Heartland.

Was it a Guardian Angel? Or was it the might of the American rescue mission that saved Captain Scott O'Grady?

We shall see. The operation that led to the rescue of Captain O'Grady was carried out after meticulous training and planning. It involved TRAP, one of the most specialized units in the United States Marine Corps.

On Friday 2nd June 1995, Captain Scott O'Grady of 555 Fighter Squadron took off in his F16 Fighter from his base at Aviano in Italy, with orders to patrol the skies over Bosnia, in order to enforce the United Nations flight ban.

Over the patrol area Captain O'Grady's F16 Fighter and accompanying aircraft, were 'locked onto' by Serb ground radar. This happened several times, and it is understood that the American F16 Fighter pilots, took evasive action; but for Captain O'Grady it was not good enough, and a Serbian Sam 6 Missile blasted O'Grady's F16 Fighter out of the sky.

Questions remain over the circumstances, in which the F16 Fighter was shot down, for normally an F16 Fighter would be capable of avoiding a Sam 6 Missile, with the use of electronic jamming and decoy chaff.

Did the F16 Fighter stay too long in the vicinity of the Serbian missile sites, after initially being tracked by Serb ground radar?

Whatever the reason, Captain Scott O'Grady was lucky to get out of his F16 Fighter without serious injury.

His luck held; for although Serbian troops saw pilot Scott O'Grady parachute to earth, he managed to find a safe hiding place before they reached him.

As the Serb troops arrived in the area where they knew he had to be, they sprayed the whole area with bullets. It was almost impossible for anyone to survive such a deadly hail of bullets; but Captain O'Grady did. Thanks, he claims, to his Guardian Angel.

"I was aware of a protective presence with me and I could hear a male voice quietly talking to me. I felt he was deflecting the bullets."

So was it more than just luck? Serb army commanders undoubtedly mounted an extensive search for the downed American pilot. A year earlier, American fighters had destroyed four Serb jets in that area; therefore, they had four good reasons, to find the American F16 Fighter pilot.

Captain Scott O'Grady believes the angel kept the Serb forces from finding him. He was certainly very fortunate to have eluded capture, during his six days in hostile Bosnian Serb territory. Only a few wooded areas interrupt the open farmland; and, the area has a large number of towns and villages, many now ghost towns.

So the odds were stacked against Captain O'Grady as he plummeted to earth.

Or were they? It is a fact that he was going to need much more than just good luck. And that he got by way of a Guardian Angel; his Protector.

Captain O'Grady was equipped only with his fighter pilot's survival kit, which consists of a life-raft, life vest with radio, flares, snare wire, seat bottom, water pump, water, first aid kit, spare radio battery, rations, axe, and bad weather clothes. All kit packed in seat bottom.

The Bell AH1 Cobra gunship helicopter, a formidable machine.

Protected by his Guardian Angel, Captain O'Grady lived off insects and rainwater, as he evaded the Serb soldiers. During the five days in which he evaded capture, he had sent signals, and soon after he made contact with over flying aircraft, he sent one more message, which said:

"Really need to get out tonight, radio getting weak." The scene was set. It was now up to the forty members, of a Tactical Recovery of Aircraft and Personnel (TRAP) team, from the 24th Marine Expeditionary Unit, on board USS Kearsarge. This was an amphibious assault ship in the Adriatic; and, with a little help from the Guardian Angel, we will soon see.

At 0008 hours on 8th June 1995, O'Grady contacts over flying NATO aircraft with his personal communicator.

At 0345 hours primary rescue aircraft launched - two Sikorsky CH53E all-weather Super Sea Stallion heavy lift troop-transport helicopters, with 41 Marines on board, these protected by two Bell AH1 Cobra gunship helicopters and two Marine Corps Harrier A V-8B jump jets. Above the helicopters and Harriers was a vast array of NATO combat aircraft; A6s, EA6Bs and EF111s to suppress Serb air defences; above them A10s and FA18s for close air support, then another layer of F16s, F15s and F18s, carrying out combat air patrol; above all these were AWACs - as seen below, this one actual used - for early warning.

One of the actual AWACs used in the operation.

At 0412 hours the rescue aircraft makes radio contact with Captain O'Grady.

At 0444 hours O'Grady marks landing site with a yellow flare, and the first to reach the F16 Fighter pilot were the two Cobras and Harriers; their role was to suppress possible ground and air attacks, and clear the way for the two Super Sea Stallions. The location had been pinpointed by an American F15 flying overhead, listening for any contact from O'Grady's personal search-and-rescue radio beacon.

A Sikorsky CH53E similar to that used to rescue Captain O'Grady.

Captain O'Grady was located between Banja Luka and Bihac, about 80 miles from the coast. He was close to a wood and at the time of rescue, it was raining and there was low cloud.

The two Super Sea Stallions put down on the marked spot and on hearing them, Captain O'Grady ran from cover. "At first I couldn't bring myself to leave cover, and make a run for the chopper," said Captain O'Grady. "But suddenly, I heard that reassuring voice saying, 'Go for it Scott, It's time to go home to your family.' I felt as if my angel was lifting me on my feet and I ran to the helicopter."

One of the Super Sea Stallions had landed on a tree stump and had difficulty lowering its rear ramp; but, as Captain O'Grady approached the helicopter, Colonel Martin Berndt, commanding officer of the 24th Marine Expeditionary Unit, and soon to be promoted to Brigadier-General, reached out and pulled O'Grady into the helicopter.

The helicopter was soon rising from the Serb controlled territory, as it did so, the rescue team came under attack from ground fire; but O'Grady was not worried for he knew his Guardian Angel would keep him safe. At 0507 hours a shoulder-launched Sam Missile was fired at their helicopter; but they were not hit. Saved by Captain Scott O'Grady's Guardian Angel.

From the killing fields to the USS Kearsarge, it was something more than just good luck, and American military might, that brought pilot, Captain Scott O'Grady back in good health.

Captain O'Grady says it was a miracle. And, after hearing his story, I must agree with him.

SPIRIT OF THE AIR HERO GHOST

R.A.F. Lakenheath can lay claim to ghosts, UFO's, and a mystery that has never been solved. I did mention Lakenheath Charlie, who has instilled fear into many on the airfield, in my book Aaargh! (This became Ghost Stations™ 2) but, since then I have received much more information, haunting information that can solve the mystery of who is haunting the airfield. But let us look first into the history of the airfield.

Construction of R.A.F. Lakenheath began in 1941 on some 2,000 acres of the Elveden Estate of Lord Iveagh, and during the Second World War, housed Numbers 149 and 199 Bomber Squadrons. Bomber Command flew 2,248 Operational Sorties from R.A.F. Lakenheath, with a loss of 85 aircraft.

In August 1948 the United States Air Force began to use the airfield for units of Strategic Air Command. The Americans took over completely in 1951. The airfield then became the home of the 48th Tactical Fighter Wing, and in 1977 they converted to the highly sophisticated, supersonic F-111 Fighter Bomber aircraft which provides, long-range all weather day-or-night nuclear and conventional air-to-surface capability. R.A.F. Lakenheath is the largest F-111 base with around 5.000 military personnel and 7.000 family members, plus a ghost or two.

Many of the ghostly sightings have been in and around the Tab Vee 46 Shelter; but there have also been many ghostly sighting and unexplained incidents around the ammo dump. Many people have reported eerie and strange happenings. Many have had footprints suddenly appear before their eyes. The Security Military Police themselves have witnessed the ghostly footprints. "It is a very unnerving experience to see footprints suddenly appear in front of you, yet no one is there to make them," said one airman who did not want to be named.

"Red Section" is the Devil Section, for this is where the haunted Tab Vee 46 Shelter is located. Red 5 Mobile Unit consisted of three Security Military Policemen, who patrolled the wooded area near the main A1065 Brandon Road. On the first patrol of their shift, they had parked behind the Tab Vee 46 Shelter and set out on their foot patrol. "We had just completed our patrol and got into our vehicle when suddenly we saw a red light at the back of us. I looked around to see a man standing a few metres away; but it wasn't a man, it was a sort of misty figure. We all felt scared and got out of there fast," said the Sergeant.

That was just one of dozens of sightings of a ghostly figure. "I was on patrol in the wooded area near the A 1065 road, when out of nowhere appears a ghostly figure. I just stared, unable to move. It moved without touching the ground. You could see it was a man; but didn't seem real, and then suddenly it vanished. I reported the incident to Central Security Control; but nothing was heard about it. It was Lakenheath Charlie I was told," said the Security Military Police Sergeant.

For the obvious security reasons, the Tab Vee 46 Shelter has been checked from top to bottom, but nothing has been found that can account for the strange happenings. "It's an eerie place to work in," said one of the maintenance people. "Tools just disappear, and the sound of organ music keeps filling the air. All is normal, then suddenly you can hear this organ music."

Over the years the notorious Tab Vee 46 Shelter has built up quite a reputation, as the most haunted place on the airfield. One night a Security MP Patrol had just checked the aircraft shelter's doors and even though securely locked, they swear they heard someone moving about inside.

Another incident was when an airman was working one night at the far end of the runway, near the 495th Tactical Fighter Squadron, when suddenly someone or something, started throwing stones at him. He quickly called Central Security Patrol.

"When we arrived on the scene we turned off our headlights so that we could sneak up on the intruder. All of a sudden we came under fire from a hail of rocks. We quickly turned all the headlight and searchlights on; but couldn't see anyone. It seemed like the rocks were coming at us from nowhere. We got out fast," said the Sergeant.

So was this also Lakenheath Charlie? It is all very mysterious. Does R.A.F. Lakenheath have more than one ghost? Many strange things have happened. Legend has it that a bomber crashed near the Tab Vee 46 Shelter during the Second World War, and all but the pilot's body were recovered. Allegedly it is the ghost of the bomber pilot who is haunting the airfield. He is the restless Spirit who has made it impossible for many to venture out alone at night.

And he could be camera shy, for when Sergeant Dave Malakoff went to photograph the Tab Vee 46 Shelter, the camera would not work. Yet it had been tested in the photo lab before going out. On checking, nothing was found mechanically wrong with the camera. Very strange. Very eerie, and very, very mysterious.

Flight Sergeant Rawdon Hume Middleton, Royal Australian Air Force, No. 149 Squadron, whose ghost haunts RAF *Lakenheath.*

Yes, it is the ghost of a bomber pilot but not the one that crashed near the airfield. After extensive research I have found that the ghost of a wartime hero, Flight Sergeant Rawdon Hume Middleton, Royal Australian Air Force, who for his outstanding gallantry, was posthumously awarded the Victoria Cross, in fact haunts R.A.F. Lakenheath.

Middleton was Captain of a Stirling bomber of No. 149 Squadron R.A.F., detailed to attack the Fiat works at Turin in Italy, on the night of 28 -29 November, 1942. On the way to target Middleton's aircraft had great difficulty in climbing to 12,000 feet in order to cross the Alps. He was forced to use excess petrol, which barely left enough for the return flight.

But Middleton was determined to continue to target, which was by now clearly illuminated by flares, and as soon as he reached Turin, he dived to 2,000 feet and made three deliberate runs over the city; facing intense fire from anti-aircraft fire in the process. But, on the third run the Stirling bomber was hit, and a large hole appeared in the port wing. The bomber became difficult to handle, next second, a shell burst in the cockpit and a piece of shell splinter tore into the side of Middleton's face, destroying his right eye and exposing the bone over his left eye. He was also hit in the legs and body. The second pilot also received head and leg wounds, which bled profusely. To add to their problems the windscreen had shattered and the bomber was almost out of control, dropping to 800 feet before the second pilot could get it back under control and release the bombs. While this was being played out Middleton had remained slumped unconscious, blood gushing from his many wounds.

As the crippled bomber, still under intense fire, limped out of the target area, Middleton regained consciousness and ordered the second pilot back to the rest station to receive first aid. The rear turret had been put out of action and the bomber was difficult to fly. Because of his severe wounds, Middleton could see very little and could not speak without loss of blood and great pain.

Nevertheless, Middleton set course for base. It had been discussed to abandon the crippled Stirling bomber, but the captain expressed his wish to reach the English Coast, so that his crew could parachute to safety. He knew that his wounds and diminishing strength would not permit him to escape unless he did so immediately.

For four hours, at a height of only 6,000 feet, the battle-scarred Stirling bomber staggered northwards. It was a long way behind the main bomber stream. Middleton seemed oblivious to the pain. Crossing the French Coast the bomber was hit again by intense light anti-aircraft fire; but determined to get home, Middleton mustered unbelievable strength to take evasive action.

By now the dying Stirling bomber roared out over the dark oily water of the English Channel, spluttering and calling out as if warning its valiant crew it could do no more. Just in time the English Coast came into view. With petrol for only five minutes flying remaining, Middleton ordered his crew to bale-out while he flew parallel to the shore. He then intended to head out to sea.

Five of the crew baled-out and landed in England, but the front-gunner and flight engineer, who had stayed to assist their gallant Captain for as long as possible, jumped too late and were both drowned. Middleton remained at the controls and at approximately 3.10 a.m. on the morning of 29 November, the badly crippled Stirling bomber, crashed in the English Channel.

It is interesting to note that from the 228 bombers despatched, 192 attacked Turin and only Middleton's bomber was lost. He was born at Waverley, New South Wales and was a great-nephew of the early Australian explorer, Hamilton Hume. Middleton's body was washed ashore at Shakespeare Beach, Dover, on 1 February 1943, and was buried with full military honours, in the churchyard at Beck Row, near Mildenhall.

But was it the body of Flight Sergeant Middleton? Very doubtful. So who, if anyone, was buried in the churchyard and lies under Middleton's headstone? An airman who was on the burial detail, said it was not the body of Flight Sergeant Middleton. So who was it? Who or what, lies buried in the churchyard?

So, could it be the ghost of Flight Sergeant Middleton looking for his other crew-members? His last wish was to return to RAF Lakenheath; and, it is strange that the ghost is always seen around the end of November! If that is true; and I think it is; then it is a wartime Hero that haunts the airfield. Is the ghost looking for the other crew or trying to solve the mystery of who is buried in the churchyard? A very ghostly mystery.

But the biggest mystery, which still remains unsolved even to this day, is the night RAF Lakenheath had a visit from Outer Space, or was it Supernatural Forces?

Two excellent pictures showing Stirling bombers of the type flown by Flight Sergeant Middleton and his crew, that so valiantly made it back to the English Coast, then could give no more.

On 13 August 1956, two Royal Air Force Ground Radar Stations detected several mysterious objects moving at high speed on a clear moonlit night.

The first Radar Station tracked an unidentified object at 4,000 feet altitude, moving westward at about 3000 miles-per-hour; simultaneously, the operators in the control tower at RAF Lakenheath, reported a bright light passing overhead toward the west; and a pilot of an aircraft at 4,000 feet over the airfield, saw the bright light streak westward underneath his aircraft.

The second Radar Station, alerted by the first, detected a stationary object at about 20,000 feet altitude that suddenly went north at a speed of around 600 miles-per-hour. The mysterious object made several sudden stops and turns, as if trying to avoid an adversary. Meanwhile, an RAF fighter had been alerted and was airborne. It made airborne-radar contacts with the object over Ely, just west of RAF Lakenheath. Suddenly the object moved around behind the fighter aircraft, at all times both being tracked by ground radar.

The fighter pilot could not 'shake' the mysterious object and a second fighter aircraft was scrambled; but, it never made contact and all radar contacts were then lost. This eerie episode was played out from 11.00p.m. to 3.30a.m; and several other radar targets were tracked in the same area and several other small moving lights were seen, but all disappeared at 3.30a.m.

This is one of the best established and most puzzling of the unexplained UFO cases. Let us remember, these strange objects were identified by radar. This measures the distance to a UFO and the direction, which may be affected by refraction of the radio beam in the atmosphere. Several effects can give false radar echoes: electronic interference, reflections from ionised layers or clouds and, reflections from regions of higher temperature or humidity, as in a cumulus cloud.

Thus, radar sightings, while more reliable in certain respects, fail to discriminate between physical objects and meteor trails, tracks of ionised gas, rain, or thermal discontinuities. Simultaneous radar detection and visual sighting in the same direction is the most reliable, but not certain evidence of a physical object.

The absence of a given explanation, as in this case, does not mean the evidence favours the extra-terrestrial hypothesis, it merely means that no explanation is known.

RAF Lakenheath was only about 5 miles - as the crow flies - from my Top Security Atomic Station. [You can read fully about the Top Secret RAF Barnham Top-Site in my book: The Avro Vulcan Adventure.]

On that particular night we did get a 'Red Alert' but no one at RAF Barnham Top-Site saw the mysterious object or reported anything unusual. I must just add that all we had to go on were visual sighting; for no need for radar equipment etcetera at my Top Security Station.

Was it just for RAF Lakenheath? Had it anything to do with the Spirit of the Air Hero Ghost?

THE GHOSTS OF FULL SUTTON

In February 1965 Peter Giles and his mate set out in their Dodge Kew lorry to deliver a greenhouse to a farm near Stamford Bridge, East Yorkshire.

Peter worked as a truck driver for Westdock Limited of Hessle Road, Hull; who were a firm of horticultural and agricultural engineers that made large sectional commercial greenhouses.

It was a dull murky day as they set out and by the time they arrived at their delivery point, it was raining very hard. By 1600 hours it was dark and by the time they had unloaded the greenhouse, all by hand and in the pouring rain, they were soaked to the skin. The farmer gave them tea, a hot bath and dried their clothes.

They left the farm at around 17.30 hours and headed in the direction given by the farmer. He had told Peter that a direct route to the A 1070 Hull to York Road; was to follow the lane for Fangfoss and Pocklington by crossing the old wartime airfield of RAF Full Sutton.

To Peter Giles it was a straight forward route; or was it? As they rolled into the old Domestic Site their powerful headlights pierced the misty gloom. The Dodge was fitted with a one-piece panoramic windscreen, so vision was very good. The truck lights consisted of two 10-inch quartz halogen headlamps; boosted by four 6-inch Lucas 'Flame Thrower' spot lights and these were all full on. They were about half way through the Domestic Site, when suddenly; into their headlight beams appeared two figures dressed in World War Two flying gear.

"I slowed down as I neared the two figures," said Peter. "They both had on flying helmets and had parachutes hanging behind. One carried a long green holdall, like a cricket bag, and as they crossed the road in front of us I noticed that they cast no shadow; and stranger still, they were not wet yet it was raining hard.

"I stopped and watched them disappear into a large Nissen Hut on my right." Peter's mate had also seen the two ghostly flyers, "Bloody Nora, did you see that," he exclaimed. Peter had seen them, in fact, he had never taken his eyes off them, and for reasons, which he cannot explain, he felt the strong need to follow the ghostly figures into the Nissen Hut. His mate did not go along with the decision and snapped: "Oh for Christ's sake let's get going." But, not waiting to hear any more, Peter grabbed a large hand lamp and dismounted from his truck.

"I walked to the Nissen Hut which had double doors and a sort of vestibule entrance," said Peter. "Once inside I shone the lamp around, but it was empty. An old iron round stove lay on its side at one end. The floor was covered in debris and some wall and ceiling panels hung loose. No sign of the two airmen." And Peter added: "No wet footprints other than mine."

Peter stood in the empty Nissen Hut that was like a time capsule and filled with all the atmosphere and Spirits of those hectic wartime years.

RAF Full Sutton was one of the last Second World War airfields to be opened in Yorkshire and became operational in May 1944, as a bomber station in No 4 Group, Bomber Command.

Full Sutton housed only one operational unit, that being Number 77 Squadron that was equipped with Halifax bombers. The last operational mission of the war came on 25 April 1945, when 19 Halifax bombers bombed the gun batteries on the island of Wangerooge.

After the war the airfield remained open for a few years and in the Fifties it housed three Thor Missiles as part of the Thor Missile Complex. RAF Full Sutton finally closed in 1963, leaving only the ghost squadrons.

"Who's there?" Called Peter. Again he called as his confidence returned. Then, he noticed another double door and a short passage to a second Nissen Hut. He found himself drawn towards the doorway and into the passage. He was unable to stop himself and he entered the second room, which had at one end a low platform and on the wall a large map of Europe.

"As I shone the lamp on the map I became aware that I was being watched," said Peter. "Not by just two pairs of eyes but many; very, very many. The feeling was overwhelming, not baleful or ill tempered, not even malevolent. Just being watched, but by someone or something I could not see."

Peter glanced uneasily around the empty room; or was it empty? He felt very disturbed and uneasy as he sensed those Spirits around him, and at that point he made a hasty retreat back to his truck. His mate was very relieved to see him and they made their way back in total silence.

Nothing like this had ever happened to Peter Giles before and the following day he told his foreman, Fred Curtis; but got a cool reception. Peter felt he just had to talk about the ghostly airmen. He had seen them yet no one would believe him.

When he told his wife what he had seen and done, she said: "I would never have dared to follow them. It is best to forget it Pete."

But Peter could not forget them. He had clearly seen them, followed them; and felt their presence. And, on thinking about the ghostly event, many questions remain unanswered.

Why were their clothes not wet, yet it was pouring with rain and his got wet? Why no shadows in the truck headlamps? There were shadows from the bushes and trees; but as the two figures crossed in front of them in the full glare of their truck lights, they cast no shadows; and why no footprints in the Nissen Hut? All so very eerie.

When I interviewed Peter Giles and asked him what his thoughts were after seeing the two ghost airmen, he replied:

"My thoughts after the event were confused. It was only after I entered the second building and the strange experience of the feeling of being watched by something I could not see, did a fear begin to arise in me."

I then asked Peter if he felt afraid on seeing the ghosts:

"Without question. No, curious," he replied. "After all the place was closed, derelict and deserted, so why should two blokes in Sid cot suits and flying boots still be around? The question of ghosts did not enter my head, perhaps I did not believe in such things, in fact. I'm still not sure I do. But, I am perfectly prepared to accept the fact that there are things on earth and in our lives that we do not fully understand."

In 1967, just two years after the ghostly event, Peter Giles was at a party and got into conversation with a man who was interested to hear about the two ghostly airmen.

"He is a very successful businessman," said Peter, "He is a Freemason and never makes a move until he consults a medium. What he said about the ghosts was most interesting. The last place called 'Home' was the airfields and the Spirit, Soul, whatever, returned there for security and peace."

Over the next few years the ghostly encounter slipped further from the mind of Peter Giles. Then, in July 1987, it happened again. Peter was delivering new paint tins for the Metal Box Company to storage for the firm of Langston, Smith and Joints.

The company had modernised a Second World War hangar at the old wartime airfield of Wratting Common in Cambridgeshire. As the truck was being unloaded Peter walked around the old airfield. As he entered the hangar he suddenly became aware of how cold it was, and that eerie feeling of not being alone, started to creep over him, just as it did that February night in 1965; but this time fear took hold and Peter quickly returned to his truck.

On seeing his frightened look the site manager asked him if he was all right. Peter then told him about his feelings inside the hangar. The site manager said he had never felt it; but added that he would not hang about after dark or go up there on to the airfield, unless he had to.

Wratting Common housed No 1651 Conversion Unit during the latter part of the war and, there were many accidents with the Stirling bomber and many crashed on takeoff.

The airfield also housed, No 195 Squadron from November 1944 to August 1945 and their four-engined Lancaster bombers flew a total of 1,384 sorties. They had many losses during their short and hectic life at Wratting Common, the worst being against Witten in the Ruhr.

It was a daylight raid to help prepare for Montgomery's trans-Rhine offensive and 195 Squadron despatched 18 Lancaster bombers. But on the way to target enemy fighters attacked them, and three Lancasters were shot down in flames. Another crash-landed in Belgium. Badly mauled, the formation continued to target, but on their return to England, No: 195 Squadron crews found that their airfield was fog bound, so eleven very tired crews had to be diverted.

The hangar that Peter Giles had wandered into was one that had been used for repairing battle-damaged aircraft; blood splattered wrecks that only just managed to make it back. Now they had gone, and only the eerie silence remains as one steps back in time.

Had Peter Giles stepped back in time that February night in 1965? Is there such a thing as a Time Zone? He certainly saw two ghost airmen; and the feeling to follow and investigate was so strong he just did so. Why? That he cannot explain. I think the reason was that Peter was on the edge of the Time Zone; but for some unknown reason, just held back.

THE HAUNTINGS AT NORTH WEALD

This story concerns North Weald, a famous wartime airfield just west of Chipping Ongar in Essex. During the war years, the station housed many famous fighter squadrons; and during the Battle of Britain, the North Weald fighters fought many a desperate battle and many brave young pilots were killed in the skies over the Kent countryside. North Weald itself became a main target for the Luftwaffe and the airfield was bombed many times.

In 1980, Denny Densham accompanied Geoffrey Croom - Hollingsworth and members of his Special Psychic Investigation Team to North Weald Aerodrome for a night's vigil in a building, which had accommodated Women's Auxiliary Air Force during the Second World War.

Denny Densham is an educated man who was a war-correspondent during the Second World War. He was not a man to be swayed by events. He had worked with Wing Commander Pickard during the making of the wartime film, 'Target For Tonight', at the now defunct Denham Film Studios, as Denny now explains for my Readers of **Ghost Stations™ 4.**

"Although most of that famous Crown Film Unit production was shot on actual locations, we managed to get hold of some Wellington bomber bits so that we could shoot some of the bomber interior with sync sound, something we could not do on location with millimetre optical sound recording equipment in those days," said Denny. "To shoot sound one needed a truck containing a sound camera and a three phase a/c supply generator and a heavy blimped Mitchell 35 millimetre picture camera," he added.

Denny Densham was in action with his movie camera after D- Day, 6th June 1944, and he was one of the first men; if not the first man, to enter Paris. He was in Malaya and a man who has had many exciting exploits. He is, therefore, a man trusted not to doctor the tapes in order to get desired results.

Denny Densham and the members of the special Psychic Investigation Team discovered that there was quite a lot happening at North Weald aerodrome. Denny – naturally – did me a copy of their sound report of the night's investigation, and in a way, this haunting parallels the Hornchurch Aerodrome haunting which concerns the slamming of doors and reported in my **original (1986) Ghost Stations™**.

The Psychic Investigation Team had been told that Building 101 was reputed and well known to be haunted; and some say it is the ghost of an airman and others say it is the ghost of an Essex Regiment soldier. Either could be true. In 1940, members of the Essex Regiment, young soldiers no more than 18 or 19 years old, guarded the airfield.

In August 1940, North Weald aerodrome received the full might of the Luftwaffe and both officers' and airmen's married quarters were severely damaged. One who was there was Squadron Leader Chippy Norton: "At the time of the air raid I was in the cook-house," he said. "I heard the air raid siren and dashed out for the air raid shelter."

In the first air raid on North Weald aerodrome there were 46 killed. An airman and an Essex Regiment soldier were trying to get into the aerodrome at the height of the bombing.

As bombs fell near them, the airman threw himself to the ground, and this saved him from the blast. The soldier was not so lucky; he was blown up into a tree and was found hanging like a rag doll.

People say it is he who haunts the building; but some people say it is an airman. The security people are adamant that it is the ghost of an airman. It is known that during the raid, an airman forgot his gas mask and he returned to his quarters for it. As he came out of his quarters, he was blown up and he was one of the 46 who were killed. Down in one shelter most of those who sought refuge were killed . . . nine being members of the Essex Regiment.

During their investigation, two members of the team got a strong smell of perfume in one of the buildings. Upstairs the smell of perfume was even stronger. The building was later identified as one occupied by WAAFs and there were some killed in that first air raid.

It was very strange how it happened. Three weeks earlier, the psychic team investigating the hauntings were upstairs in the building, when all of a sudden; one of them got an overpowering smell of perfume. He thought it was after-shave lotion and turned to the others in the group and asked them if anybody had used any after-shave. They all said: "No. Why?" Suddenly two of the group got a strong scent smell. They put it down as being a Brylcream smell. It was only afterwards that they found out that it was a WAAFs building that they had been in that night; and it could well have been scent. The smell was only for about a minute or so, as one of the group said: "You sort of walked through it. I picked up the smell of scent, but by the time you had walked back, the smell had gone."

The building they were in was dilapidated and there was nothing there that could have produced the smell of scent. After two separate incidents of smelling the strong scent aroma, they decided to investigate it further. It was much more than just a coincidence.

After many inquiries, they found a woman who cleaned at the aerodrome and they went to interview her at Ongar. It was established that in 1968, the York, Lancashire Regiment moved in and they encountered really grim experiences on the old wartime aerodrome - door slamming and other ghostly noises - which were reported in the newspapers.

The woman cleaner brought her friend in who was also a cleaner at the aerodrome. It was their job to get the place ready for the soldiers to move in. They were working in a room when all of a sudden they heard furniture moving about upstairs. I would just like to add, the buildings were locked when the cleaners entered and locked when they left. They unlocked the buildings when they arrived in the morning. So no one could have been in the buildings. When the two cleaners heard all the noise upstairs, they were very disturbed. "Who the devil is upstairs throwing things about after we have just polished the damn floors," said one of the cleaners. With that, she dashed upstairs but there was no one there.

The second occasion happened two days afterwards. They were busy cleaning when the same thing happened. Banging upstairs with noise of furniture moving. They again dashed upstairs to find out what was going on; but this time, besides hearing noises of moving furniture, all the dormitory windows had been thrown open.

In 1979, Epping Forest District Council purchased some of the buildings, mostly the hangars, and one evening at dusk, Mr. Mike Bailey, the officer in charge of the museum, was going across to hangar 1, when he suddenly looked across and he was amazed to see a phantom airman stood near the hangar. He thought he was seeing things and he looked again, and sure enough, there stood an airman. Suddenly the phantom airman vanished. This was in September 1985.

Two nights later, he was again going into hangar 1, at about the same time, six-thirty in the evening and, as he looked in the direction of where he saw the phantom airman, he saw not only the airman this time but also two WAAFs and another two airmen stood behind. He thought he must have been going barmy. So he looked again and there they were. The thing that he was struck by was the fact that they were all dressed in uniforms of the 1940 period. And, they all looked very miserable and unhappy. He could not get away from the expression on their faces.

The building selected by Denny Densham and the Special Psychic Investigation Team, was a wartime two-storey Accommodation Block that had been used by the Women's Auxiliary Air Force during the last war. Downstairs was the original air raid shelter. "We went into the original air raid shelter," said Denny, "more for nostalgia purposes than anything else, because as far as we understood, this part of the building wasn't haunted."

Fortunately, Denny had switched on his tape recorder as they walked down into the shelter and it provided some mysterious material.

For Denny Densham, it brought back many nostalgic memories and it was exactly as he remembered wartime air raid shelters. "Apart from some rust on some bedsteads, it might have been as if we were waiting for an air raid," he said.

As they started to make their way back up, Denny paused at the top to tap on the steel, bomb-proof, anti-blast door, and when he played back the recording, he found to his astonishment that one channel on the recorder had got a lot of interference on it. "You can actually hear the interference," he said "there is no explanation what caused this interference and it didn't occur again for the rest of the evening, in fact, it hasn't occurred on that machine since. That is another mystery." And, he added: "So very often when you are doing psychic investigations with electronic equipment, something goes wrong with it and you can actually hear this breaking through on the left channel and I have no explanation for what caused that interference."

I have Denny Densham's tape and have played it over many times, but cannot solve the mystery. I can hear on the tape someone saying 'mind your head' and Denny saying 'Steel Doors rusted up.'

Before they started their investigations, Denny Densham and the other members of the team did a thorough search to make certain that there was no one else in the building. "I had two, reel- to-reel, portable recorders with me," said Denny. "So I left one running upstairs and carried the other one around with me." Denny continues: "We made our camp at the far end of the building and while we were in there, we suddenly heard the sound of a door slamming and, there was no accountable reason for it."

Fortunately, Denny had his tape recorders running and they picked up, very clearly, the sound of a door slamming. I have heard the tape. It is an eerie sound but clearly that of a door slamming in an empty sounding building.

At the time they heard the ghostly noise, Denny did not know if the tape recorder upstairs had picked it up. "We have just had a bang of a door and we are not quite sure where it is located," said Denny. "What the hell was that?" said someone near Denny. Then Denny is heard to say: "I hope the machine upstairs picked it up." He went on to say: "I will just try and see if we can find a door that could have done it. All these doors are open and that one is an outside door which is locked." Sounds of the investigation team can be heard on the tape as they try to solve the mystery of the slamming door. "Now wait a minute, we went into the toilets just now," said Denny, "and that door was open." "Was it?" asked someone. "We went through, don't you remember," cut in Denny. And he continued: "We went through here just now." The tape recorder continues to pick up the conversation and noise of their footsteps as they look around the building. One can get the feeling just listening to the tape that it is in an empty building and eerie, from the shuffling effects of their feet. Denny is then heard to say: "That is odd. We came through here because I said" Just at that moment someone is heard to say, "Here, wouldn't be that."

There is then a confusion of conversation as the adrenalin begins to run high. "Now wait a minute. We came in and walked right through," said one team member. "Is that a lavatory? Did you go to the front door?" "No." Then Denny is heard to say: "Because I made the remark as we came in that there was pee places for men, which seemed unusual for WAAFs."

It was all so very strange. All the other doors were open and the only one that could have made the noise was locked; but this could not really have accounted for the noise for there were no other doors downstairs that showed any sign of movement. Satisfied that the slamming did not come from any door downstairs, they then went and explored the next floor of the building. The tape recorder with Denny was kept running all the time. He is heard to say: "Going upstairs now," then footsteps on the stairs and voices as they make their way to the next floor. At this stage, Denny stops to ascertain that the tape recorder was still running. "Yes, it is still going." Denny is heard to say. They then continued their way down the corridors to see if they could solve the mystery of the door slam. However, while they were walking down the passage they heard another door slam and this was picked up by the second machine, but this time, the slamming sounded more distant for they were now some distance down the passage.

The tape recorder picked up very clearly the noise of a door slamming, someone is then heard to say in a frightened voice "Hey, where's that?" I do have the original recording made on the machine that Denny was carrying on his shoulder. The team members are heard walking along and discussing possibilities as to what caused the door slamming. Hey, now where is that come from, it was along here wasn't it?"

However, despite a very careful search of the entire building, the only door that seemed to have moved was the one by the downstairs lavatory, but to add to the mystery this door was apparently locked. All the other doors were open and there did not seem to be any sign of movement from them.

Denny Densham summed up their nights work: "The thing remained a mystery," he said. "Quite obviously, we had had two doors slam during our night investigation there and no explanation for it."

But there was one other rather curious event during their investigation. In the room right at the end of the building where the Psychic Investigation Team had made their headquarters, a place to regroup and to have their coffee and sandwiches to sustain them during their night's vigil, they had set up some candles.

Denny Densham explains: "There was one candle burning by a window and the window had lost some of its glass. One would have expected that the draught from outside would have blown in.

"We found, to our astonishment that the candle flame was blowing over, and bowing towards the window, as though the draught was coming from inside, and yet, the building was otherwise more or less sealed up. All the other windows in the building were shut; in fact, this was the only broken window in the building. I made a remark about it at the time."

On the master tape that I have from Denny Densham, he did indeed record the eerie sensation of the candle flame. Denny is recorded as saying: "There is a draught coming now, but it is coming the wrong way. It is coming from inside the building and blowing our candle flame towards the window instead of coming the opposite way. The draught should come through the window from outside." The other members are mystified at what Denny had pointed out to them and they all converge near the candle. "The draughts going the other way," one is heard to say. "Is there a door open?" asked another. "Let us sort out where the draught is coming from," Denny said. But once again, they had no answer to the mysterious candle flame.

"It is rather unfortunate that the Barrack Block and the adjoining ones have now been pulled down and the aerodrome is being taken over, I think, by light industry; so we shall not be able to continue investigating on that particular location," said Denny Densham, and he added: "But it does show that strange things do happen in old aerodromes."

THE GHOSTS OF HENDON

Hendon circa 1912. The public loved the air-shows and those men in their flying machine … and still do.

'Hello there', came a voice from behind the Flying Boat, as the two wardens started to ascend the stairs at the far end of the building. 'Hello there,' said the voice again, very clearly and in a rather posh accent. 'Hello there,' but there was nobody there. The voice repeated the greeting 'Hello there', at which point the two museum staff at RAF Hendon ran up the stairs in a state of near panic. A thorough search of the area was made. But there was nobody to be found.

Many ghostly stories have come out of Hendon Museum and the new Bomber Command Hall has only increased the strange and eerie happenings. It is easy to understand why, for the museum is a very emotional place, and at night it is very easy to let one's feelings run wild. One night two cleaning ladies saw a man in overalls smiling at them from the top of a scaffolding tower. They reported it to the warden for the workmen had long since gone home. The warden investigated and found nothing. A few days later the mystery figure was seen again on the scaffolding.

One night in the Battle of Britain Hall one of the night security staff was walking past the German Me110 and out of the corner of his eye, thought he saw a pair of boots walking along behind this aircraft, near the wall. He turned up the lighting and went upstairs to get a better view of the hall, called up some assistance and carried out a through search, but nobody was there, just an eerie atmosphere.

Hendon dates back to 1909 and the first aerobatic and parachuting displays in Britain were held at Hendon. The 1920s and 1930s were the golden years for Hendon. The airfield was sold to the Royal Air Force in 1925, and during the Second World War Hendon housed many fighter squadrons. The airfield was attacked many times. A flying bomb hit a wing of Colindale Military Hospital and four airmen were killed. Another flying bomb exploded in front of a brick Barrack Block in the southeast corner of the airfield on 3 August 1944, killing nine airmen and injuring twenty-five.

By the autumn of 1945 all units had moved out, including the Air Ambulance Unit, which had been based at Hendon since 1942, leaving behind only the ghosts.

During the 1950s housing development gradually encroached upon the airfield until it became unsafe for flying.

Today, Hendon aerodrome has almost gone and only the memories remain. To keep alive those memories one hangar is still in use as the Royal Air Force Museum. The museum was established in 1963 and is sited on ten acres of the historic former Hendon airfield. Steeped in history, it is understandable that ghostly happenings are widely reported, ghostly voices, faces; and figures that just disappear. Is Hendon the largest Ghost Station in England? To find out, a Para psychic Group decided to spend a night there. It took place on the Saturday night and Sunday morning, 19-20 March 1988. The following is a report of their vigil by the Chairman of the Ghost Club, Tom Perrott:

'We were dispersed in pairs throughout the building. Mark and Ron manned the Red Base Post. The Clarks were stationed at Green Base in the middle of the Aircraft Hall, while Jock and myself at Yellow Base, occupied the area by the Nissen Hut. John had the whole area of the museum to range with his video camera, but as it happened on this occasion, did not succeed in photographing anything unusual.

'During the course of the vigil the following incidents were alleged to have occurred:

'At about 9:30 p.m. Angie felt as though she was struck firmly on the top of the head by a clenched gloved fist, while she was standing near to a Hawker Hart biplane.

'At about 10:00 p.m. Mark, while returning to base along the upper gallery, heard a loud bang, as if something had been thrown down. Despite an intensive search, nothing tangible was found.

'At approximately 2:00 a.m. I drew Jack's attention to the fact that the cockpit of one of the fighter aircraft appeared to be lit up, and through the transparent cupola covering it, could clearly be discerned what appeared to be the silhouetted figure of a helmeted pilot's head. On closer investigation I found that the illumination was the reflection of the museums overhead lights and the dark silhouette was the headrest behind the pilot's seat.

'At about 4:02 a.m. an apparent 'cold spot' was felt by the Clarks accompanied by a tingling sensation, as of a galvanic current, which could be felt in the fingers.

Just as Mark and the Clarks had entered the Bomber Command Wing at about 4:20 a.m. a vivid flash of blue light was seen to cross the wall beyond a Lancaster Bomber. At the same time the atmosphere became distinctly colder and a small radio microphone succeeded in picking up the sound of a non-metallic object falling in the vicinity, followed a little later by a metallic crash. It would be as well to mention here that during the construction of the museum, three building workers had fallen to their deaths by falling through the glass roof.

Hendon during the golden years. An air display in 1928. The aircraft on the left is the Supermarine Schneider Trophy machine.

'While Jack and the Clarks returned to their respective bases, Ron and I carried out a brief watch in the vicinity of the Halifax bomber. It was then that

Mark, who had been strolling around the gallery, claimed that he saw a human figure, which appeared directly between a Typhoon and a Tempest aircraft, gliding across the kerb in the direction of a tubular maintenance gantry. He said that the figure, which soon disappeared, seemed to be stooping, was clad in black and seemed to be faceless.

'The final two occurrences took place at 4:22 a.m. when a sudden metallic crash was heard by five members of the party. Shortly afterwards Mark, while walking near the centre stairs, believed that he felt a light tap, as if from a single finger, on the top of his head. At 4:32 a.m. there occurred one of the strangest manifestations of the whole vigil, in that all members of the party, with the exception of Ron and myself, who at that time were in a different part of the building, distinctly heard a very loud humanoid groan, which appeared to come from the entrance area of the Aircraft Hall. There was no rational explanation for this.

'There were no further happenings and we all departed at about 7:00a.m.'

After his vigil in Hendon Museum, Tom Perrott said: "Whatever is the answer to the strange happenings which, undoubtedly took place during the hours of vigil, my psychic appetite has certainly been whetted."

Is the old airfield at Hendon a Ghost Station? Does the Silent Few sweep by at night? Many people think so. Why not pay a visit to the Royal Air Force Museum and the Battle of Britain and Bomber Command Museums and find out. 'Hello there!'

THE FICKLE FINGER OF FATE

We have just seen how superstition was very rife with most aircrews, Just before operations, a wrong word could be fateful for the superstitious crew members, this was very much so for Flight Lieutenant Charles Ellis of 467 Squadron, Royal Australian Air Force, based at RAF Waddington in Lincolnshire.

On the night of 1st/2nd February 1945, Bomber Command scheduled a raid against the town and marshalling yards at Siegen, just east of Cologne. A total force of 271 Lancasters, of which, 22 aircraft were from 467 Squadron, were detailed for the attack

"My regular crew weren't flying that night," said Flight Lieutenant Ellis. "Flight Lieutenant Keith Livingstone's rear-gunner in Lancaster G-George went sick, and as Squadron Gunnery Leader, it was my responsibility to nominate a replacement gunner; and I nominated myself.

"Because it would be the last trip to complete my second tour of operations and Flight Lieutenant Livingstone's final trip to complete his crew's tour, I jokingly said to Ray Browne, the mid-upper-gunner, prior to briefing, with a coincidence like that we are a 'moral' to get the 'chop' tonight."

At the briefing, the Intelligence Officer informed the assembled crews, as was the practice during that stage of the war, not to take risks in the event of being shot down over Germany, as the end of the war was imminent.

Over Siegen, low unbroken cloud spoilt bombing conditions. However, during the bomb run, the bomber crews aimed at sky markers laid by the Pathfinder Force, which rapidly became merged with the glare of incendiaries.

Lancaster G-George, with Flight Lieutenant Ellis on board as their rear-gunner, made its bombing run, and was just pulling out of the target area when the intercom crackled into life. "Bomb-Aimer to Skipper, there is a thousand pound bomb 'hung-up' in the bomb bay." But before the Skipper could answer, G-George rceeived a direct hit in the starboard wing, and the starboard engine burst into flames.

Flight Lieutenant Charles Ellis - second on left, the one leaning on the propeller.

The German night fighter had attacked them without being seen. Charles Ellis had not seen any fighters from his rear-turret so; it would appear the attack had come from the front of the aircraft; but that was not so.

A German night-fighter using a pair of 20 millimetre cannon mounted in the fuselage and. arranged to fire upwards and forwards, which enabled the night-fighter to attack from below, had in fact hit the Lancaster. This was the blind spot for the bomber crews and, an area they could not defend.

For Flight Lieutenant Ellis the attack came as a shock: "The next thing I remember is the Flight Engineer saying: 'where is my parachute?'" he said. "The Skipper called over the intercom and said 'looks like we've had it chaps, you'd better bale out.' I was wearing a 'back' type parachute, and turning the turret, got out into the fuselage. Upon going forward, I met the mid-upper gunner who had already jettisoned the escape hatch. The flames from the fire in the engine and probably the wing fuel tanks were streaming down the side of the aircraft. Ray Browne said:

Close-up of Flight Lieutenant Charles Ellis, Royal Australian Air Force

"You bastard Ellis, you've 'mozzed' us." He then turned

and disappeared through the escape hatch. I followed suit and the next thing I knew was a welcome jerk on the parachute harness, which indicated that the chute had opened. While descending, I could still hear Ray, who was of course floating down below me, saying: 'you bastard Ellis.'

"I saw the burning G-George pass underneath me and then it appeared to turn back on another course; and the thought flashed through my mind, 'Hell, the Skipper's attempting to fly back to base and leave us in Germany.' I was not to know at the time that the Skipper, was apparently endeavouring to control G-George, but his gallant efforts were to be of no avail as the aircraft crashed and he died with her."

Charles Ellis still had Ray Browne's words ringing in his ears as he plunged into a deep snowdrift. He quickly snapped out of his parachute harness and buried it, together with his parachute and flying suit, in the snowdrift. It was only later that he realized that he had left his escape kit in his flying suit.

After a cold night spent in a train carriage, Ellis was taken prisoner. Over the next two days the remainder of the crew were rounded up, making a total of seven, for G-George had been carrying a Second 'Dickie' Pilot, and this apparently had satisfied the Germans for a normal Lancaster bomber crew was seven.

After a spell at the Interrogation Centre in Frankfurt the crew were then taken to a holding centre at Nuremberg and marched to Stalag V11A Moosburg, north-east of Munich from whence they were eventually liberated by the American Army.

The Skipper, 155465 Flight Lieutenant J. K. Livingstone, DFC, RAF, was killed over Siegen on 1st February 1945 whilst pilot of Lancaster NG197 of 467 Squadron. He was originally buried at Rengsdorf Cemetery; however, in 1948 his body was transferred to Rheinburg Military Cemetery.

Members of the crew who became prisoners of war were: 102110 S/Ldr O. O. Sands OSO, OFC, RAF (Navigator) 53553 F/O E. G. Parsons OFC, RAF (Flight Engineer) 412818 F/O W. O. McMahon RAAF (Bomb Aimer) 182270 P/O J. Pendegast RAF (Wireless Operator) 172986 F/O R. N. Browne RAF (Mid-upper Gunner) 418931 F/Lt E. C. Ellis RAAF (Rear Gunner)

432138 F/O R. W. G. Eagle RAAF (Second Pilot)

Had Flight Lieutenant Charles Ellis put the Fickle Finger of Fate on the crew of G-George? It makes one think that was so; for from the twenty-two crews that set out for Siegen, only Charles Ellis and his crew failed to return. It was the Fickle Finger of Fate that decided their destiny.

CALL IT SUPERSTITION

Just about all wartime aircrew were superstitious. They were addicted to, or swayed by, superstition by the very nature of their duties, the darkness, and the high loss of aircraft and aircrew made them superstitious.

For the wartime aircrews, it was a practice resulting from the fear of the unknown, not from ignorance. For some, mysterious circumstances gave way to ghosts and the supernatural; many had good cause to be superstitious.

But superstitions, in some cases, are inseparable from religious superstitions and this was very much so with many of the aircrews. People develop personal superstitions and the aircrews were no exceptions.

Nearly all persons, in all walks of life throughout the ages, have held seriously, or half seriously, irrational beliefs concerning methods of warding off bad luck, foretelling the future, and healing or preventing sickness or accident, for the wartime bomber crews it was good-luck needed for a safe return and for a tour of Operational Sorties.

To bring them good luck, many of the aircrew carried what they contended to be lucky charms, one of the most notable belonging to Flying Officer C. E. Smith, who flew Halifax L V907 NP F (Friday the 13th) on 29 Operational Sorties. Smith sported a real air force type 'Handlebar' moustache and he always carried with him on each mission a large white toy elephant, some 18 inches tall. The elephant was called 'Dumbo', and remained in the cockpit beside Smith at all times. This earned him the nickname of 'Dumbo' Smith.

Halifax pilot, Doug Bancroft, always insisted on having his cap hanging on the emergency hydraulic pump lever - why, he cannot explain - just superstition - did it once and was lucky; so had to continue. It was just lucky to do so.

Another bomber pilot would put on a Navy Captain's cap as soon as the bomb aimer had said the magic words – 'Bombs Gone'. As soon as the pilot heard that, he put on the Captain's Cap and started to climb out of the target area, as he did so, he started to sing "A Life on the Ocean Waves" weaving the bomber from side to side as he did so; and this was a sign for the rest of the crew to join in. They had done it once and were lucky so they continued. They survived the war. For that crew it was lucky. Very Lucky.

Elsham Wolds, a bomber airfield situated in north-east Lincolnshire on the bleak Wolds, was home for No. 103 Squadron from the day it opened in July 1941, until November 1945. The code letters allotted to No. 103 Squadron during this period were 'PM'. The squadron flew Wellingtons, Halifaxes and Lancaster bombers. By the time the Lancasters arrived, it was soon evident that any Lancaster with the identification letter 'A' Able, had a jinx on it, in fact, it was more than a jinx; 'It was the Evil Eye' as someone put it.

The first Lancaster coded PM 'A' Able was shot down within two weeks. Another 'A' Able quickly replaced it; but within a few days, it had gone missing.

Air Crews were now looking on any Lancaster coded 'A' Able with great superstition; and after a few more losses, someone said: "No more 'A' Able as an Identification Letter." To make up the Identification Letter for the whole squadron, they had one squared, an example being Lancaster ED701 PM-B². But the best example was Lancaster ED888 PM-M² (Mike Squared), which did more operations - a total of 140 - than any other aircraft in Bomber Command. Their rewards for such outstanding service … the scrap heap.

Lancaster PM-M² (Mike Squared) was a 103-Squadron aircraft, and with the Identification Letter 'A' Able removed because of superstition, maybe that is how Mike Squared came into being, it proved lucky for all the aircrews that flew in her.

But sometimes, unlucky omens worked in reverse and brought good luck, the best example being Halifax LV907 NP-F, Friday the 13th, of No. 158 Squadron. Halifax 'Friday the 13th' proved to be very lucky for all who flew in her and the Halifax Bomber set up an Operational Record in just - appropriately - 13 months it completed 128 Operational Sorties. Friday the 13th was so called, because its nose and fuselage were painted with superstition-defying ill omens; such as a skull and cross-bones and an inverted horseshoe. On the fuselage, over the door, a ladder had been painted and the navigator sat in front of a cracked mirror. Sadly, the gallant aircraft failed to save itself and it was reduced to scrap soon after the war. The bomb-log panels of Friday the 13th were salvaged; and today, are on display in the Royal Air Force Museum at Hendon.

Dogs were considered lucky and most aircrews had a dog of some kind. They were very superstitious about their pets; a good example of this is with Bobby. This was a half-breed retriever-Shetland sheepdog that latched on to an aircrew at Royal Air Force Ludford Magna, on the Lincolnshire Wolds. The dog and bomber crew were inseparable, and it went with them in the crew bus out to their Lancaster bomber on the dispersal pan. As the crew boarded the aircraft, Bobby would make straight for the trailing wheel and urinate on it. The crew laughed as Bobby cocked up his leg. It brought them good luck the crew said. Then one night in January 1945, a new driver of the crew bus would not allow Bobby to get inside. He raced across the snow-covered airfield, but was too late to add his little pee-ce of luck; Sadly, the bomber failed to return and the crew has not been heard of even to this day. After waiting patiently for its masters aircraft to return back to base, Bobby suddenly gave a little bark and dashed across the airfield never to be seen alive again. His body was later recovered in a snowdrift and the airmen buried Bobby by the side of the road. The ghost of Bobby has been seen many times around the old airfield at Ludford. The weather was very bad, it was very cold and it had been snowing hard. Did the crew take-off without knowing that Bobby had not blessed their trailing wheel? Bobby knew it and that is why his Spirit still roams the old airfield of RAF Ludford Magna today.

Superstition reared its ugly head in many ways. Women sometimes wore the badge of superstition as Stan Holtham recalls: "When I arrived at Elsham Wolds, I crewed up with a new crew and on my first day out with one of my crew, I saw this beautiful WAAF. She was a little doll. I looked at my crewmate, who had been on the airfield a few months, and said; "I'm going to enjoy it here at Elsham with girls like that." "Stay away from her, Stan. She's a Chop Girl, he said."

There was also a WAAF in the Education Section at Elsham Wolds, very beautiful, but no one would go near her. These were girls whose boyfriends were either killed or went missing; 'got the chop' was the term used. Word soon got around the airfield, which girls were bad luck and usually the aircrew would keep well clear of them. They became known as the 'Chop Girls.'

The finger of superstition could point at anybody, anything or any place. This became so with the village of Bracebridge Heath near Lincoln. Just after the war, married quarters on some RAF Stations were very hard to come by. "This was very much so in 1948/49 when I was posted to RAF Waddington," said Stan Holtham. "There was a village called Bracebridge Heath which was close to RAF Waddington and the people there were willing to put us up. But no one would ever go to live in the village because all the chaps who had digs there were killed. We lost an awful lot of men who were on Lincoln bombers during my time at RAF Waddington."

Superstition for a Christian, many believe that in time of trouble he will be guided by the Bible if he opens it at random and reads the text that first strikes his eye. Many did read the Bible and pray before a mission, but to be doubly sure, many would take along that special silk scarf or the lucky button or rabbits foot.

ADDITION

This File brought forth a flood of superstitions and it is impossible to relate them all here. As previously stated, just about all aircrew were superstitious and everyone could relate some mysterious happening. But, not always to do with the supernatural … or was it? Take the case of Flight Sergeant Bill Perry, who was a wireless operator with a bomber crew of No.51 Squadron: "The only unexplained thing that I can recall, that happened during our tour, was during a return trip from Germany," said Bill. "Something hit the front of our Lancaster bomber, with quite a thud, at a height of over 5,000 feet. On landing we inspected the Perspex nose and found a gory splodge on it, which appeared to include some hair or fur."

So, you may say, nothing supernatural about a bird strike, even though night-time. Certain birds do fly at night; but at over 5,000 feet. A very strange encounter. Had they zapped Count Dracula?

One bomber pilot, Wing Commander Reg Stidolf, always made a right hand turn, never a left, after completing the bombing run and coming out of the target area. If they were attacked, it was always a right hand corkscrew turn they made first; and it paid off for them, their superstition worked, for they survived the war. That is what they believed, that the right-handed turn was their good luck.

That was a very strong belief with many wartime aircrews, and they may be right in that belief, for after all, you always turn right to pray. Offerings are made to the Gods with the right hand. You salute with your right arm - longest way up, shortest way down - Oaths are sworn with the right hand. In marriage ceremonies, the right hands are joined. A Holy place should be entered right foot first. So, Reg Stidolph's right hand turn out of the bombing area, kept him and his crew in favour with the Gods.

They had done it once and survived; so they continued to do so; and it became a sort of ritual for Reg Stidolph and his crew.

But why the right? Could it be that the left is associated with Evil and bad luck? It is true to say that if greedy Spirits of the dead need placating by a gift it is always given with the left hand. Also, left-handedness marks a possible sorcerer; and sinners leave the church by the left door.

Superstitious beliefs are very deep rooted in history; and ancient customs and practices grew around the aircrews, for they could not afford to have bad luck on board with them. They needed all the Good Luck they could get.

LOST FOR A KISS

Despite what they may say to the contrary, most Royal Air Force aircrew, were superstitious in one way or another; and, readers of Ghost Stations™ will understand why from previous stories. On 28th September 1944, Flight Lieutenant McCuaig prepared for a routine photographic reconnaissance sortie; his orders, to photograph the Focke-Wulf aircraft factory near Bremen in Germany.

Bremen, Germany's second largest port, had last come in the bomb-sights of RAF Bomber Command on the night of 18th-19th August 1944, when its heavy bombers showered the port with 1,130 tons of bombs and incendiaries.

At this period of the war the allies had massive air power, and for Flight Lieutenant McCuaig it was indeed a very routine sortie. He was a very experienced pilot and left nothing to chance. Every time before a mission he would shower and before putting on his dog-tags (identification disc), he would kiss them for good luck before putting them around his neck.

Flight Lieutenant Duncan McCuaig, aged 24, was a photo-reconnaissance pilot, Stationed at RAF Benson in Oxfordshire. At that period of the war there were two Spitfire PR Squadrons, No.541 and 542, one of their pilots being McCuaig; and two Mosquito PR Squadrons, Nos. 540 and 544.

The RAF had a most efficient Photographic Reconnaissance Unit, thanks to Sidney Cotton, who during the early part of 1940 got some perfect pictures from 33,000 feet.

To give PR aircraft the edge over the enemy fighters, all excess weight, which included guns and gun fittings, were removed. So although the aircraft were unarmed, they did have an added advantage, which in the hands of a skilled pilot, proved to be no problem against enemy fighters.

By the summer of 1944 the Benson Spitfire PR Squadrons had a few Mustang 111's and had just received the first of the Griffon-engined PR MK XIX Spitfires. These were the photographic - reconnaissance version of the Mark XIV with wings modified for additional fuel. Rear-view hood; universal camera installation. Maximum speed 460 miles per hour with a ceiling of over 43,000 feet and a range of 1,500 miles. These figures are very important, as you will see as the story unfolds.

Flight Lieutenant McCuaig was soon airborne and heading for his target, the Focke-WulfFlugzeugbau factory. It was an uneventful flight to target and with pictures taken, he was soon heading back to base.

Suddenly, for some unknown reason McCuaig's photo-reconnaissance Spitfire, became the target of two German fighters; ironically, both Focke-Wulf 190 D-9's, the components of which had more than likely come from the very factory that McCuaig had just photographed.

McCuaig's luck was running out and running out fast. Why? And why was such an experienced photo-reconnaissance pilot caught unawares? That I will explain in a moment.

Flight Lieutenant McCuaig fought to regain the advantage; but it was too late; one Focke-Wulf was now in a killing position a few seconds later the PR Spitfire was in flames and spinning earthwards out of control, after being raked by 30 millimetre cannon from the lone Focke-Wulf. It crashed to earth, killing the pilot. So what had gone wrong with what should have been a routine photo-reconnaissance sortie?

Hauptmann Robert 'Bazi' Weiss, the German fighter pilot who shot down Flight Lieutenant McCuaig. Weiss himself was killed in aerial combat with Spitfires on 29-12-1944 near Lingen.

One, Duncan McCuaig's Spitfire was obviously caught at a disadvantage, despite the fact that it was faster (remember the figures?); it had maximum speed of 460 miles per hour, the Focke-Wulf FW 190D-9 had a maximum speed of only 440 miles per hour at 37,000 feet. The PR Spitfire of McCuaig had a ceiling of well over 43,000 feet. So could have flown all the way back to base, well out of danger of all enemy fighters.

So why did it not do so? That I will answer in a moment let me first give the second reason for going wrong.

Two; of all the German fighter pilots to come up against, Duncan McCuaig came up against one of Germany's best, none other than Hauptmann Robert Weiss, also aged 24 and Kommandeur of the 3/JG54 Squadron. Hauptmann Weiss was holder of the Oak Leaves to the Knight's Cross of the Iron Cross. Not a man to have on your tail when your luck is about to run out. Duncan McCuaig became Weiss's 119th kill.

And it had nothing to do with the fact that Flight Lieutenant McCuaig's Spitfire was unarmed. All photo-reconnaissance aircraft were unarmed which gave them the extra speed and height to keep out of trouble.

So what went wrong? The answer is simple. Duncan McCuaig took off from RAF Benson without his dog tags. For some unknown reason he did not put them on. He should have been wearing them; but he was not doing so. That means he failed to kiss them for good luck, for he never put them on. That explains why his luck ran out.

Superstition? Call it what you will. It is a fact that Flight Lieutenant Duncan McCuaig always kissed his dog tags for good luck before putting them on; and, it is a fact that the only time he did not do so, he was shot down and killed.

And it is a fact that his PR Spitfire should have been flying well out of harms way, well above the deadly cannon of the single-seat Focke-Wulf FW 190D-9; but it was not doing so and he paid the price. Lost for a Kiss.

THE DEVIL'S QUOITS

As the air war intensified, more and more airfields were needed to keep pace with the rapidly expanding Royal Air Force. It was decided early on in the war, that the eastern side of England would house the Bomber Stations, the south to house the Fighter Stations and the midlands and western side would be used for Training Stations. One such training airfield was Abingdon, in Oxfordshire, which was built during the RAF expansion period in the 1930's.

Within a few months of war being declared, RAF Abingdon was bursting at the seams with aircraft, and it soon became apparent it would need a satellite airfield. Many sites in the area were surveyed and the final choice was an area just west of the village of Stanton Harcourt.

But the chosen site brought problems; not from difficulties with the landscape, but from the three large stones standing in a field that would soon be turned into an airfield.

When the villagers learned of the RAF's intention to build an airfield near their picturesque village, and in the process knock down the three large stones, they were horrified at the suggestion not at the thought of the airfield; but at what they were going to do with the three large stones.

As one villager said: "Did not the Royal Air Force realize that those stones were the Devil's Quoits; and if they disturbed those stones it would mean death, and the accident rate on the airfield would be high."

The RAF planners scorned the superstition and announced that the airfield would be built where planned. But to please the villagers, they gave orders that the 'Devil's Quoits' were to be set flat under the runway.

"Beware, the curse of the Devil Quoits," cried the villagers as the civilian workmen arrived with their machines, and commenced work on turning the green and pleasant fields into an airfield. The workmen laughed at the superstitious villagers and set about their work. They had an airfield to build and no superstitious stones would stop them.

The airfield quickly took shape and as the days passed, the workmen thought less and less about the death threat regarding the Devil's Quoits. The three large stones still stood there, everyone knowing that who disturbed the stones, it would mean death. But surely for only those who believed in the superstition.

Men had just started work on laying the runways, when suddenly; death fell out of the skies. On 16th August, 1940, three German bombers, "one for each of the three stones," said the locals; dropped out of the sky and attacked the workmen working on the new airfield.

The German aircraft bombed and strafed the men as they ran for cover. As the dust settled, five workmen lay dead; and another four died later of their wounds.

Was it the revenge of the Devil's Quoits? Nine died, three for each stone, three stones, and three lives each.

So, those who disturbed the stones, brought death, as the superstition said; but that did not stop the work and the airfield opened as a satellite for Abingdon; and for the duration of the war, it housed No. 10 Operational Training Unit.

The airfield closed after hostilities ceased and parts of the old wartime airfield became a quarry.

In the late 1970's, Stan Galloway returned to Stanton Harcourt for a stroll down memory lane. During his break between his first and second tour with RAF Bomber Command, he was posted to Stanton Harcourt, in 1942, as an instructor with No.10 Operational Training Unit.

He had only been on the airfield a few days when he heard the story about the Devil's Quoits. That was a long time ago now; but it was still very clear in Stan Galloway's mind as he drove down the entrance road to the perimeter track.

"From the perimeter track all I could see was the conversion of the airfield into a quarry, and no signs of the Devil's Quoits, he said. "I drove along the perimeter track until I came to the old control tower." And, he added, "I just had to explore inside it."

The wartime control tower - the keeper of memories - was in good condition and had braved the elements very well. Stan made his way upstairs and on to the balcony, stirring up a spot of nostalgia in the process.

After a short time, he made his way back down the stairs and to his car. He was just about to get in, when a farm-worker shouted to ask what he was doing on the old airfield.

"I apologized for trespassing," said Stan, "and explained that I was stationed at Stanton Harcourt during the war. In the course of conversation, he asked if I had been in the control tower.

"He was surprised to hear that I had been inside. He then told me a young Flying Officer, who had been killed in a flying accident, haunted the control tower. He said no one in the village would go in the building, so strong was the superstition."

Had the Flying Officer, like the others, disturbed the Devil's Quoits and paid the ultimate price? Yes, I think so. However, I also think that the villagers' used the warning, as a method of defence, for keeping trespassers at bay.

Maybe it was superstition; but I also think that there was something, such as the denoting power of the Devil's Quoits.

THE PHANTOM OF SQUIRES GATE

During the late 1950s, Miss Julia Wolfe-Harlow was at Squires Gate Airfield, on the southern outskirts of Blackpool, as a trainee airhostess and employed by Mr Russell Whyham.

It is one of the oldest airfields and flying goes back to 1909; but it was not used during the First World War. The airfield was taken over by the Royal Air Force during the Second World War, and it opened with No.3 School of General Reconnaissance in December 1940. This unit remained the main user throughout the war.

Throughout 1941 the airfield housed many Night Fighter Squadrons with Defiants, and many were in action during the raids against Merseyside.

One famous personality that was at Squires Gate was Amy Johnson. She took off from the airfield in an Oxford on 7 January 1941 and, is said to have crashed in the Thames Estuary; but her body was never recovered; and remains one of the mysteries of the Second World War.

On the edge of the airfield was a shadow factory for Wellington production; and between 1940 until the end of the war, over 2,500 Wellington bombers were built at Squires Gate. When Miss Julia Wolfe-Harlow arrived the airfield was back in business with general aviation.

When she was not in the air as a trainee air hostess, Miss Wolfe-Harlow spent her time at a pleasure flight-booking kiosk across the large field.

One particular wet day she stood in the booking kiosk watching the rain pour down. "Suddenly I turned and looked towards the door," said Miss Wolfe-Harlow. "Standing against it and with his arms folded, I saw a young man who was staring ahead of him. 'Hello, I didn't hear you come in,' I said, but he didn't look at me. He was wearing some kind of light grey uniform, but no cap - but what was so strange was the fact that his clothing was quite dry. As I stared at him - suddenly recognizing him - he disappeared!"

Some time later Miss Wolfe-Harlow told her colleagues about the incident and one of them said, "I don't wonder you recognized him because that was Neville Duke, he was killed about two weeks ago!"

Today Blackpool Airport is a busy airport and many of the wartime buildings still remain.

PLEASE NOTE. Miss Julia Wolfe-Harlow's colleague was wrong with regard to Neville Duke, who was thankfully very much alive and well, as you will now read …

My previous story, 'The Phantom of Squires Gate', brought a flood of mail to inform me that it could not have been Neville Duke who Miss Julia Wolfe-Harlow had seen as an apparition.

Mr. F. A. C. Roper, from Weybridge, even took the time and trouble to send me a photocopy of the relevant page for Duke, Neville Frederick, from the current edition of Who's Who.

Mr Roper wrote: "You write about Miss Julia Wolfe-Harlow who claimed to have seen the ghost of Neville Duke, I enclose a page from the current Who's Who which may interest you. It was of great interest to me for Neville is a very good friend."

Indeed Neville Duke has also become my very good friend; and, let me have his wartime photographs … plus a special signed photograph for me. Some of his photographs are published in my Italy book.

So, who had Julia seen?

Now, we know that it was not Neville Duke. So, who was it that Julia saw? - I did receive a few suggestions - Mr. E. T. Manby from Lincoln was one of the many who wrote to me and he said:

"In the 'Phantom of Squires Gate' you describe how Miss Wolfe-Harlow recognized the figure of Neville Duke who was 'killed about two weeks ago'. I rather think she must have been mistaken for in the late 1950's Neville Duke; a near neighbour of mine at Dunsford was very much alive. Could it have perhaps been John Derry, another very well known test pilot, who I am sure you well remember, was killed when his aircraft broke up as it was turning behind the control tower during the 1952 Farnborough Air Display."

I then asked Julia if she could have been mistaken - for it could not have been Neville Duke - she replied:

"As for your question, it was very definitely Neville Duke that I had seen. This was confirmed by quite a few of the staff who heard my description of the young man - and, although we bought a daily newspaper, we did not see mention of his death two weeks back. At the same time, it is said the 'phantoms' of existing people can be seen, when they are still alive."

So, Julia was still adamant that it was indeed Neville Duke - It could not have been. So who was it she saw?

I asked Neville Duke and he said: "Rest assured no harm done by premature announcement in your book. It has happened at least once before - in Australia."

Neville then went on to say: "I did visit Squires Gate a lot during my time as Chief Test Pilot with Hawker Aircraft when they built a factory there for the production of Hunter aircraft. Looking through my log books I started flying up there in April 1952, from Langley, using the company Rapide and made the first flight of a Squires Gate Hunter in May 1954.

"My visits went on until 1956. I did go into the Air Traffic Building to book in and out, as was the practice in those days, and I think the pleasure flight kiosk was in that building."

So on the plus side, we know that Neville Duke did fly in and out of Squires Gate Airport; and, he would have to pass the pleasure flight kiosk, but gladly in the flesh I might add.

I then asked Neville if it could have been whom Mr. Manby suggested: "John Derry was killed at Farnborough on 6th September 1952 - I am sure he had no connections with Squires Gate." he said.

So we are back to Square One. The mystery remains and, to give you food for thought, Squadron Leader Neville Duke, wartime pilot - Desert Air Force, holder

World Speed Record 1946, World records: London-Rome, 1949; London-Karachi, 1949; London-Cairo, 1950; World Speed Record, September 1953 and Chief Test Pilot, Hawker Aircraft, seen in the photograph below that he sent to me, said:

"For what it's worth … I do have a habit of standing with my arms folded!"

SAVED BY THE GHOST OF HIS BROTHER

Pilot Officer Jimmy Corfield, 2nd right, front row – the elder brother who was killed in August 1941

Bill Corfield had just one ambition - to be a bomber pilot in the Royal Air Force like his elder brother, Jimmy. As a sixteen-year-old schoolboy, he looked up to his brother when he was home on leave in the early days of the war; and was proud to see his brother in uniform. In a kind of way it was a sort of 'Biggles' hero worship. Yet, in those dark early days, bombing was in its infancy, and aircraft were very poor.

Pilot Officer Jimmy Corfield was a pilot with No. 21 Squadron at Royal Air Force Watton in Norfolk, flying Blenheim Ivs; and during the early part of the war the squadron played a prominent part in No.2 Group's offensive against shipping in the English Channel and the North Sea. It was a most hazardous occupation attacking daylight targets on low-level strikes.

Jimmy could see the hero worship in his younger brother each time he was home on leave, and knowing the odds of survival were very slim, he tried his best to put him off joining the Royal Air Force as a pilot. "You're not cut out to be a bomber pilot so try the other Services," he told his younger brother many times. But, Bill would mutter under his breath and it only made him more determined to be a pilot. If his brother could do it, thought Bill, then he would also. "We might even get to fly together if the war lasts long enough," Bill used to say excitedly to his elder brother who would smile and shake his head.

"Things are so different Bill when you are up there with flak all around you - fear grips you, and you haven't got the right temperament."

"It doesn't matter," said young Bill. That was to be the last conversation he had with his brother Jimmy.

On 12 August 1941, 54 Blenheims attacked an industrial factory outside Cologne. It was a daring raid and it was the first time that so many aircraft had bombed the heartland of Germany in daylight. It was not only meant as a boost to morale but also to aid the Russians in relation to the German advance.

The raid had been carefully planned and No. 21 Squadron had gone to RAF Bicester to practise bombing on an area near by, similar to their Cologne target; No. 452 Squadron escorted the Blenheims and their task was to divert enemy fighters to help Bomber Command's heavy daylight attack. Sadly many were hit and among the missing were Jimmy Corfield and his crew.

Three weeks later news was received that their bodies had been washed up on the island of Texel in the North Sea, near the coast of Holland. Bill was just 17 years old when he heard his brother was killed in action; and the news made him more determined than ever, that he wanted to be a bomber pilot and carry on where his brother had left off. He owed it now to his brother Jimmy who had played such a big part in his life.

In July 1943 Bill Corfield was called up. During the interview many wanted to be fighter pilots, which was glamorous and all the rage, but not Bill Corfield.

"My brother was a bomber pilot," he said, "and I want to be a bomber pilot. It is all I have ever wanted to be, and now I have my chance."

After being selected he went to No. 28 Elementary Flying Training School at Wolverhampton, and then to RAF Cranwell. After training on twin-engined Wellington Bombers at No. 82 Operational Training Unit at RAF Gamston in Nottinghamshire, Bill Corfield then went to No. 1654 Heavy Conversion Unit at Wigsley in Nottinghamshire. This was a four-engined Lancaster Conversion Unit and was responsible for accepting personnel from OTUs; and then, after four-engined familiarization and training, turning them out as complete crews for the Squadrons of No.5 Group. But, the war was now at an end and there was no need for bomber pilots, so, Bill Corfield was posted to Royal Air Force Desborough, Northamptonshire and flew Dakotas with No. 44 Group, Transport Command.

In 1946 he was posted to No.1 Ferry Unit at Pershore in Worcestershire, and began ferrying various types of aircraft overseas. In January 1947, Flying Officer Bill Corfield, was detailed to fly a brand- new twin-engined Anson 19, serial VL307 to Singapore.

He got together his crew for the long journey, Flying Officer Wally Wright; navigator, and Flight Lieutenant Johnny Stoker as his wireless operator.

The Avro Anson had a service ceiling of 18,000 feet and a maximum speed of 178 m.p.h. at 7,000 feet. It was a bomber/reconnaissance aircraft and also used for transport and training. With no load it had a still air range of 730 miles and to everyone was known as old Limping Annie.

It was snowing when Bill Corfield and his crew took off on 13 January 1947, and the Anson climbed slowly into the winter sky on its first leg. They flew to Buk just outside of Paris, then to Lyon. After refuelling on to Ciampino near Rome. The next leg took them to Naples where they stayed overnight.

On the morning of 21 January, they set out across Italy to Bari where they again refuelled to make sure that they had enough fuel to cross the Strait of Otranto to Athens. The direct route would take them over the Pindhos Mountains, which are over 8,000 feet, and to be safe they would need to fly above 10,000 feet. They were not equipped with oxygen or de-icing gear so it was decided to follow the coastline. So far Bill Corfield had flown at an average height of 5,000 feet.

As they crossed over the heel of Italy and headed out across the Strait of Otranto the crew chatted and had a few sandwiches for lunch. In clear blue sky they headed down into the Ionian Sea and over the Ionian Islands.

After two hours they began to run into the electric storms that had been forecast en route. Within minutes they were being buffeted by strong winds and ahead of them huge cumulonimbus clouds began building up.

Bill Corfield could tell from the feel of the aircraft that it was more than just a local storm and he asked his navigator for a radio fix. They were flying at 5,000 feet and visibility was deteriorating rapidly. The electrical storm was giving problems for a radio fix and it was also forcing them down.

They were past the point of no return and Corfield knew that his only chance was to head straight through the storm. The little Anson tossed around, as Corfield was forced lower and lower, amid thunder and lightning. Suddenly, they caught a glimpse of the coastline and decided to follow it.

It was their only chance. Rain lashed the Anson and it took a beating as Corfield fought the controls. He knew what loads were imposed on airframes and the little aeroplane must be at its limits. The violent buffeting would have done damage if he tried to climb, so he had to stay only 50 feet above the waves. The cloud base and the sea almost merged. They were now on a wing and a prayer - and to add to their problems fuel was becoming critical.

They followed the coastline along the Gulf of Corinth, keeping a sharp lookout for the coastline ahead, and then straight across to Athens, or at worst, if they could not climb, ditch on the shore. At 50 feet they were too low to get a radio fix, so they had to rely on visual identification.

Suddenly the navigator shouted, "I see the Corinth Canal." It was a chance, thought Corfield, and he had to take it - at least in the canal the storm would not be fierce. With that he steered the little old Anson towards the huge gash carved through solid rock over 250 feet high, which is the Corinth Canal. It is four miles long and only 80 feet wide and it separates mainland Greece from the Peloponnesus. To give an idea how small it is, only one ship can pass through at a time.

The shelter they expected from inside the canal was not forthcoming and Corfield thought it was the end. The rain lashed mercilessly and the altimeter was holding at 50 feet. The wipers could not clear the windscreen, and the wind was so violent it was like being in a wind tunnel. Any mistake now and they would be dashed to pieces against the rock sides.

On the other side of the canal lay the Saronic Gulf and Athens; but for the Anson crew they were not through the canal yet ... they only had a few feet to spare for the wingspan of the Anson was 57 feet. Now they had entered the canal there was no turning back. Everything went dark, rain lashed the aircraft and Bill

Corfield sat tense at the controls. He was sweating profusely.

Suddenly Bill Corfield had a feeling of peace and calm and he released his tight grip on the control column. "I felt that someone had joined me in the cockpit," he said. "It was an invisible force in the second pilot's seat. During this period the compass was completely still and at that point I said 'Hello Jim' in my mind." The Anson was flying itself and all was peaceful and quiet. Unseen hands had taken over the controls.

F/O Bill Corfield

Bill Corfield knew who was in the second seat; he did not have to look. "It lasted about four minutes … it was utterly natural," recalls Bill Corfield. Seconds later they were out of the canal and the darkness gave way to another world. The crew cheered:

"You've done it Bill. How the hell I shall never know," said Johnny Stoker. They both remarked how calm and quiet it was in the canal.

Some minutes later they saw the lights of Athens through the rain and not before time, for the fuel gauges were almost at zero.

After one circuit they were down, and as they taxied along the runway, the port engine suddenly spluttered, went 'putt-putt' and cut out.

For Bill Corfield, he knew who to thank for saving their lives. He had always told his brother he would fly with him and he knew it was Jimmy who had come to his aid; at the time he needed him most.

Jimmy Corfield is one of 168 laid to rest in Denburg Military Cemetery, on Texel Island. Was it Jimmy Corfield, who returned to save his younger brother?

Bill Corfield has no doubt it was; and I know that he is certainly right. His brother was by his side all the way.

BIRCHAM NEWTON REVISITED

"I have a follow-up to the Bircham Newton recording which will fascinate you," said Denny Densham. How right he was. Denny knew of my interest in Bircham Newton aerodrome. I said in my other book that of all the 'ghostly airfields Royal Air Force Bircham Newton had to be at the top of the ghost league. The aerodrome was active in both the First and Second World Wars.

Briefly, let me retrace a few of the main ghostly encounters at one of the most haunted aerodromes. Mary Tock was a WAAF nursing orderly at Royal Air Force Bircham Newton who had a ghostly experience in 1949. Decades later it still chilled her as she related it to me.

There were many other hauntings reported at the old wartime airfield but the most puzzling is the haunted squash court, which was built during the First World War. Many people have heard ghostly footsteps in the viewing gallery. Also many people have seen a ghost airman in the viewing gallery.

One of the most psychic recordings ever made was from the haunted squash court. The tape recorder picked up the sound of muffled speech. And, a ghostly woman's voice can be heard . . . most spine chilling.

I have the actual tape recording and it is most frightening, when one knows it was recorded in an empty squash court. The tape recorder picked up metallic clangs and noises as though heavy objects were being moved around. It was an unearthly, eerie sound, and it gave the impression, that one was listening to the everyday sounds of people working in a hangar in wartime. No one could explain the sounds on the tape. And everyone who visited the haunted squash court said they had an uneasy feeling, and felt cold when in the right hand court.

To try and solve the mystery of the haunted squash court a couple called Sue and Jeffrey Cooper, who live in Bishop Stortford, decided to do a follow-up on Denny Densham's original investigation.

They went down to Bircham Newton and they actually got permission to spend the night in the squash court. They entered the left court and they found it had a perfectly normal atmosphere but, when they went into the right court, there was just something curious about it; something strange, which fascinated them.

They had a cassette recorder with them which they put on the floor of the building and they actually stood around and waited, while they were recording. Now, they did not hear anything themselves, but the recorder picked up very similar sounds to the sounds that Denny Densham recorded.

I do have both tapes from the recordings; and in the second tape, the one recorded by the Coopers, you can hear odd thumps and there was again a metallic ping, rather fainter than the one that Denny recorded; but nevertheless, a metallic ping. There was also a metallic clank, but there was nothing in the building that could have caused that sound. The walls are lined with timber and the end walls are brick with a plaster surface that was used to hurl the ball at when playing squash. At the other end of the building is a wooden gallery; but nothing metallic, so it is a mystery as to how these metallic sounds were caused.

"Even more mysterious is the way you get these very heavy clanks," said Denny. "It is the only way I can describe them. It is rather like heavy objects being moved around and one might imagine them inside an aircraft hangar."

To hear the tape one is left in no doubt that the sounds are those of a wartime hangar. The tape recorder picked up one sound that was quite remarkable for it could well be the sound of an aero-engine. It went on for about twelve minutes and towards the end, it sounds as if the engine revs up, for the tone of the engine changes.

There is no way this particular sound could have been produced inside a completely empty squash court. I have heard the tape recording and I have to agree that it clearly sounds like an aeroplane engine on run-up in a hangar. Denny Densham said: "For my choice, I would say that that was a piston engine, or a twin-engine machine, that is standing on an apron with its engine ticking over; and the changing tone towards the end of the recording seems to add some authenticity to the sound. How it came about I just don't know."

Another mysterious sound on the tape recording the Coopers described as a hangar door closing. But again, there is no logical explanation for what it really is.

"It could be a hangar door closing," said Denny. Towards the end of their tape they got what apparently are footsteps going down the staircase from the minstrel gallery; ghostly footsteps. I have listened to the tape recording and one can clearly identify footsteps. It does seem that there is something going on in the squash court, although I am completely baffled by how these sounds can be recorded."

Everyone is baffled. The haunted squash court did not yield up its eerie secret. It is another game to the ghosts of Bircham Newton. The ghosts in eternal time.

THE CIGARETTE GHOST

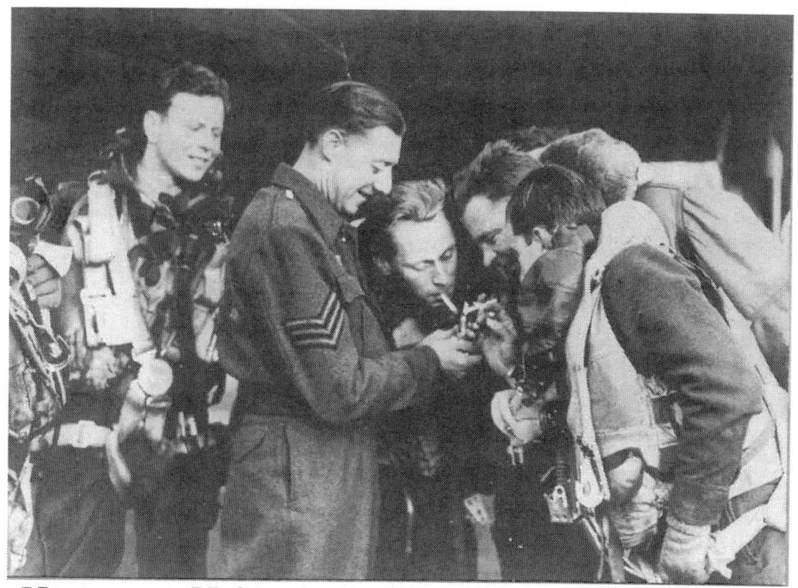

Here we see a Halifax bomber crew getting that welcome light on their return from another mission. The Sergeant always waiting for the crews with a light for that first cigarette.

Many stories lie dormant in the mind and are triggered by some unexplained event; a tune, a picture or, in the case of Stuart Chapman, a book or should I say books, to be more correct. I will let him explain in his own words:

"Reading Military Airfields of Yorkshire and the Ghost Stations™ series, I was reminded of my days as a National Serviceman in the Royal Signals during 1948-50; following Basic and Trade Training at Catterick I was posted to the former RAF Bomber Station

Pocklington, then known as No.2 Depot Regiment Royal Signals, later becoming The Depot Regiment Royal Signals.

"Then, in August 1948 the airfield was in a reasonable state, the main landing strip and perimeter track being in good condition. The control tower was located on the far side of the field, close to the village of Barmby Moor; on the B 1246 road and I remember a 'J' type hangar near to the Admin Block on the opposite side of the field.

"At that time Royal Signals personnel volunteering for parachute training, would assemble at Pocklington for primary physical and parachute training, prior to jumping and qualifying for parachute wings at Aldershot, the perimeter track was used by them for endurance running and speed marching, whilst the main runway being utilised for the dangerous practise of rolling from the tailboard of a moving truck whilst attached to an open parachute to simulate the effect of landing. This was later banned due to the number of injuries sustained.

"The main runway also made an ideal pitch for many games of fast and furious army hockey. Apart from this the only exciting period was during the summer of 1949 when a Spitfire made a forced landing on the main runway having run low on fuel. The pilot was duly whisked off to the Officers Mess for tea and crumpets. The following day a petrol bowser arrived from RAF Driffield and our Spitfire duly departed.

"There were rumours of a ghostly figure of an airman usually seen at night in the vicinity of the hangar, and this figure would request a light for his cigarette; and, in the glow of the match would be seen an RAF pilot complete with brevet and flying gear who would then vanish.

"Another report said a member of the guard had seen a blazing Spitfire in the hangar, at this time the hangar doors had been closed for security as our MT Section was housed therein. It was said that this guard's hair turned white overnight.

"I never experienced the apparition myself, although I slept in the Admin Block adjacent to the hangar on numerous occasions. What I do remember vividly, after all these years, is the ghostly and erne way those hangar doors used to creak on those cold Yorkshire nights.

"My memory was also jogged by Ghost Stations™ IV, page 116, left stranded by the roadside at Stamford Bridge after a night out in York by a cab driver who said that Pocklington was just across the fields.

"I stumbled across a deserted and lonely airfield which I now know to have been Full Sutton - Ghost Stations™ III. I eventually arrived at RAF Pocklington in the cold light of dawn. Thank God it was Sunday."

The above story proves two points, one, it was the books that triggered the memory; and two, not everyone sees a ghost or are affected by supernatural surroundings.

It is also true to say RAF Pocklington was, and still is, haunted, even though it closed in 1946 and most of the wartime buildings have been removed. For many decades the control tower remained but it too has now gone. The hangars remain and are listed as grain stores.

The cigarette ghost has been seen many times, each time requesting a light for his cigarette, and upon receiving a light would vanish. It is thought to be the ghost of a Halifax bomber pilot that crashed in the area.

And it is true that a guard's hair turned white overnight after seeing what he thought was a blazing Spitfire in a hangar. Ghostly and True.

THE FRONT LINE PHANTOMS OF RAF HAWKINGE

"I am not a terribly superstitious or imaginative person," said Mr Clifford Dray from Densole, Hawkinge. "But what I heard that August night in 1982, as I passed the site of the old Hawkinge airfield, sure made my blood run cold."

This hilltop site some two miles north of Folkestone in Kent was first used for aviation as early as 1910. The aerodrome opened in October 1915 as No. 12 Air Acceptance Park, with few facilities other than three canvas Bessaneaux hangars.

For the rest of the First World War building work continued and in 1920 Hawkinge became a fighter station, a role that it retained for most of its active life. Over the next two decades the facilities were improved by the construction of brick-built barrack blocks, messes, workshops and other buildings.

On the outbreak of war in 1939, Hawkinge then became a recruit training camp but by the early part of 1940 this unit had been moved and replaced by operational squadrons.

Hawkinge was in the thick of it from the start with its squadrons attacking the advancing German armies; and when France fell, work started on protecting the airfield against the expected German attack.

The aerial assault began in July 1940, and for several months the airfield was at the centre of some of the fiercest fighting of the Battle of Britain. The airfield buildings took a battering with all but one of the hangars having been destroyed by the end of the summer.

Hawkinge remained a very active airfield, housing a succession of squadrons until the end of 1944. The majority were Spitfire squadrons, but seven squadrons were equipped with Hurricanes.

By the end of 1944 urgent repairs were needed to the war damaged buildings and airfield surface; however, by that time the war was approaching its closing stages. A new generation of warplanes was just beginning to come into service, powered by jet engines and needing large airfields with concrete runways. Hawkinge was totally unsuited for this new breed of aircraft; so it began to run down and was put on a Care and Maintenance basis. In July 1947 some of the buildings were occupied as a WAAF depot; and for a short period, there was gliding from the airfield.

During this period a ghostly fighter pilot was reported on the airfield late at night. "He was dressed in flying kit and wearing a flying helmet," said one WAAF; and she added: "He had a sort of eerie glow and as I watched him he just vanished."

There have been many other reports about the lone fighter pilot who appears to walk sideways as if wounded. "The figure was greyish and had a sort of hazy look about it," said another person who had seen the phantom fighter pilot on two occasions.

Some people thought that the phantom fighter pilot was one of the Battle of Britain pilots who was killed when his Spitfire crashed near the airfield.

With its lifeblood drained, RAF Hawkinge closed in December 1961. The little grass airfield that had seen Service in two-world wars stood silent; but it has not remained silent, for the unmistakable sound of a Spitfire, has been heard over the airfield where the Kent Battle of Britain Museum now stands.

Clifford Dray had been to visit a friend who lives on the new estate in Hawkinge, which is directly opposite the Spitfire leisure drome, which was an old aircraft hangar.

"It was just turned 10.30 p.m. on 14 August and it was a misty sort of night; and as I reached the gates to the museum I clearly heard an aircraft engine," said Mr Dray. "I thought it must be a generator on the aerodrome but it was all locked up and I couldn't see any lights. I got a short way down the road and the engine seemed to rev higher, and I can only describe it as an aeroplane taking off."

Mr Dray was very puzzled for it was clearly an aircraft taking off from the old airfield, which had long since closed - the last fighters being in 1945. "My blood ran cold, and I had mixed feelings of extreme excitement and a nervous feeling in my stomach," he said. "I say a nervous feeling because I can't remember having felt it before." He added, "I can't explain it away with simple logic."

The front line phantoms of RAF Hawkinge are restless; and are they restless because they won the war but lost the peace?

Battle of Britain fighter pilots of 'A' Flight, 32 Squadron take a well –earned rest at Gibraltar Road Dispersal at Hawkinge, September 1940. From left to right: Pilot Officers Smythe and Proctor, Flight Lieutenant Brothers and Pilot Officers, Grige, Gardner and Eckford. Those are the valiant young men who fought for our freedom.

THE WINTER GARDENS CHILLY ENCOUNTER

The Midland Hotel is not the only haunted building in Morecambe, so too is the Winter Gardens Theatre.

The Winter Gardens Theatre at Morecambe - 1993. Closed since 1977

The grand, ornate and mighty Winter Gardens Complex was requisitioned by the government in 1939 and, was used for a variety of uses which, included training for the RAF and also to entertain the thousands of RAF personnel.

Back of the Winter Gardens Theatre. Thousands of airmen were drilled on this car park

The old Winter Gardens Theatre has a long history dating back to before the turn of the century. And Morecambe has a long history with the military that goes back to the First World War. It housed the military in the First World War and, when the troops left in 1916, the town was filled with munitions workers who, were engaged at the National Projectile Filling Factory at White Lund on the eastern edge of Morecambe.

Most of the workers were women who could earn up to £5 a week, which was more than twice the peace-time rate for men. During this period, shops in Morecambe did a roaring trade in £10 fur coats … No anti-fur protesters around in those days. And with such a trade in fur coats, thus was born the expression …

All fur coat and no knickers.

For undoubtedly many of the munitions girls did their bit for the troops and thanks to the many 'soldiers farewells', Morecambe's birth-rate reached the national average.

During the Second World War Morecambe was considered a safe area, hence the reason why the Midland Hotel became an RAF Military Hospital. The town and area also became home for hundreds of evacuees and civil servants whose numbers totalled 5000. The civil servants were billeted in Morecambe and their offices overflowed into hutments on Oxcliffe Road. All of these plus the Royal Air Force.

The gardens at the rear of the Winter Gardens (now replaced by a car park), was used by the RAF and, was where the recruits did their physical training … better known to millions as PT. Sadly, PT is now a thing of the past, even from schools, gone the PT lesson, replaced by drugs and the like as society slides down the sick and slippery slope, to the madhouse.

There are many, many ghostly stories surrounding the Winter Gardens Theatre at Morecambe, one very interesting one concerns a workman who was working on the stage one night. The theatre was empty … or so he thought, for he suddenly heard clapping from the gallery.

Who or what was the phantom audience he did not know. Was it the airmen from the semi-circular room with the windows built into the wall with candles for daylight, at the Midland Hotel?

Are they the phantom audience of today? During the war the Winter Gardens Theatre was filled to capacity with civil servants and the Royal Air Force who came to see all the big names in show business - Billy Cotton and his band, Henry Hall, Joe Loss, Vera Lynn, Jimmy James, George Formby - they have all been to the Winter Gardens, not surprising as it was regarded as the Palladium of the North.

RAF *show at Morecambe in 1993*

In 1962 the Black and White Minstrel Show packed them in at Morecambe. The list of artistes who appeared is endless.

Now all is gone for the Winter Gardens Theatre closed in 1977 and, in 1982 the ballroom building adjoining the theatre was demolished.

Now only the ghosts of yesteryear remain … Morecambe's ghostly past. And it is interesting to note that one of those who took part in the 'Final Performance' of the last show at the Winter Gardens Theatre was the Central Band of the Royal Air Force.

THE WHITE ELEPHANT GHOSTS

Despite it being totally unsuitable as an airfield, RAF Acaster Malbis in Yorkshire, opened in January 1942 under No. 12 Group, Fighter Command.

The airfield was in such a bad position, I could not believe it possible; but it was, and I – repeat, I, BBH, have named this airfield the 'White Elephant'

The first and only fighter squadron to be based at Acaster Malbis - the White Elephant - was No. 601; and they were flying the new American Bell Airocobra Fighters. But major technical problems, bad weather; and the fact it was at the White Elephant; caused many crashes.

On 12 February 1942, one crashed in the River Ouse and the pilot was drowned. With the unsatisfactory state of both airfield and aircraft, the squadron moved out after only ten weeks.

Being unsuitable as a Fighter Station, Flying Training Command took it over; and the Oxfords of No. 15 (Pilot) Advanced Flying Unit took up residence. But this unit also lost aircraft due to misty conditions along the River Ouse. The mortuary was becoming a very busy place.

The obvious signs that it was not suitable as an airfield were ignored; and, unbelievably, the site was then developed into a Heavy Bomber Station.

The whole area is nothing more than drains and dykes; yet construction work started, and Acaster Malbis was rebuilt with three concrete runways. It was complete with two 'T2' hangars and hutted accommodation for the personnel. The bomb dump was to the east of the airfield.

The airfield opened under Bomber Command; but wisely, it did not receive any operational bomber units. Then some bright spark - who did not have to fly from the White Elephant - thought it was suitable for training, and it was subsequently transferred to No.7: (Training) Group; and the airfield was used by aircraft from nearby Heavy Conversion Units.

The White Elephant airfield finally closed in early 1946. The site continued in use until the early 1950s.

From mid-1949 until early 1951, W. Hayes was at Acaster Malbis during his National Service, as a Ration Storeman.

"There were many rumours that the Decontamination Centre was haunted by aircrew in flying gear," he said; "apparently it had been used as a mortuary."

One airman said that he saw an airman in flying gear step out of the mist and then disappear before his eyes. "It was always when there was a mist," said one airman, "a slight drone could be heard and many people saw phantom figures in the mist."

THE PHANTOMS OF RAF KIRTON-IN-LINDSEY

In early 1944, LAC Eric Hilton Hewitt was posted to RAF Kirton-in-Lindsey in Lincolnshire. He was under training for General Duties; and, eventually became responsible for station discipline, after two years and three months on the station. The airfield had opened as a Fighter Station in May 1940; and the first three squadrons were Nos. 222 and 65 with Spitfires and 253 with Hurricanes. It then housed many fighter squadrons with Belgium, Free French, Dutch; and Australian Air Force, Polish and American pilots with the first American Eagle Squadron.

The role of the station was to give fighter cover to the Northern Sector, fly convoy patrols off the east coast, support Circus Operations; and provide for-battle-weary squadrons to rest up and re-group. The airfield came under attack from the Luftwaffe in 1940 and 1941.

One night in August 1944, a chum in the next bed, who seemed scared out of his life, awoke LAC Hewitt. "Listen," he said; "can you hear anything?"

"I sat up in bed, straining my ears," said Hewitt, "sure enough I could hear some rather garbled French - but where on earth was it coming from?" Hewitt was very puzzled and jumped out of bed to investigate. They searched all around with torches – "We could hear screams and still more voices in French," said Hewitt, "but could find nothing."

The next day Hewitt mentioned the incident to an airman who had been at Kirton-in-Lindsey since it had opened: "Ah yes," he said, "One of the barrack blocks was hit during a raid. It was Block 37 which at that time was occupied by Free French pilots - there were many killed."

In 1965 the station was finally vacated by the Royal Air Force and transferred to the Army, housing the Royal Artillery. There have been many unexplained sounds and one person reported hearing unearthly screams and another seeing a phantom wartime fighter pilot near one of the hangars.

THE FRUITLESS SEARCH

With a splutter, the engine stalled and the aircraft plunged to the ground, and burst into flames. Defiant L 6982 had been on a Meteorology Flight and while approaching to land, for some unexplained reason, the nose went up and the engine stalled.

A flight mechanic who was first on the scene said, "The pilot, Squadron Leader Ingham, was beyond all aid; and the gunner, Pilot Officer Maggs, was severely injured. The engine had been torn from the airframe and also the turret, with Maggs in it."

One who heard the crash was Leading Aircraftman 'Junker' Joyce, who was in the Station Armoury at the time. It was July 1940, and he had just been posted to RAF Warmwell in Dorset, after completing an armourer's course at RAF Manby in Lincolnshire.

The equipment of the Central Gunnery School (CGS) was Wellington 1s and 1As, Hampdens, a Miles Master, a Boulton Paul Defiant and two or three Fairey Seals, which vanished soon after he got there.

The Defiant had crashed within the airfield boundary and the turret, which was wrenched from the aircraft in the crash, was brought into the armoury with gore all over the gun breech cases. "I can still see the wreckage; and smell it," recalls Joyce.

A few days after the crash there was a Station Parade on the aerodrome when the ashes of Squadron Leader Ingham; were scattered over the airfield from a

Wellington bomber flown by Squadron Leader P. Haynes.

The airfield opened in May 1937 as a Training Station. The object of the CGS was to instruct air-gunners with Squadron Service into the latest techniques in aerial fighting.

Warmwell was divided into two parts, the domestic and technical areas. In the latter were the hangars, crew rooms and all the many sections making up the station.

During the summer of 1940, 152 and 609 Squadrons used Warmwell. The latter flew in from Middle Wallop in the morning and returned home just before dark. The Battle of Britain raged over the Kent countryside; but by 27 September the worst of the aerial fighting was over.

Throughout the past few weeks there had been many rumours started about Squadron Leader Ingham's ghost. It was said it would visit the Flight Office and change the flying rosters. It was very scary for the night Duty Crews; and it was said that some had heard the noise of a Defiant taxiing out.

One night in early December, LAC Joyce was Duty Armourer; and with this duty, it entailed sleeping in the armoury office.

It was a bright, clear crisp night; and about 6.30 p.m. he left the NAAFI and headed to the Armoury Section. This consisted of two rectangular huts with a concrete path between them. One hut was the workshop and the other contained the administrative offices, at least one half did, the other half was the bomb carrier storeroom.

The only entrance to the office part was a door opening to a hallway giving access to four offices formed in a square around it. The first was the office of the Armament Officer, which was always locked at night. The next office was that of the Central Gunnery School Armoury; and that would be home for LAC Joyce until relieved-in the morning. Across the small hallway was the office of Mr. Frank Waters of Vickers Armstrong, Weybridge. It had formerly belonged to Squadron Leader Ingham. The fourth office was that of the Station Armoury, locked since the cessation of work.

LAC Joyce had the keys to all the offices and the key to the outer door. Outside there was no sound save an old Local Defence Volunteer (LDV) guard, coughing and hawking on the tarmac not far away. The LDV was the forerunner of the Home Guard, and were usually old soldiers, that had been issued with uniforms and rifles at the outbreak of war. Experience had shown that the LDV guard was hard to get rid of, when they dropped in for a natter and a bit of shelter.

So LAC Joyce carefully locked the outer door straight away and then tried all the other offices to make sure they were locked. A single blue bulb lighted the hall; blackout screens covered all the windows.

"I wanted an early night," said Joyce, "I had had a very busy day, so I wrote a few letters before turning in." For a short while he lay reading *Men Only* of 1940 vintage.

"I was just about to drop off, when much to my surprise, I heard footsteps coming down the concrete path to the outer door, the door opened and someone came in, walked across the hall to the door of Mr Waters's office, opened it and went inside - then all was quiet."

Joyce sat up in bed spellbound: "Am I dreaming?" he whispered to himself. "No I wasn't, I had heard someone open the outer door, cross the hallway and whoever it might be was now in Mr Waters's office.

"A sudden thought struck me; the doors had opened – but no key had been used -. I had checked the doors myself and only I had the keys to them.

"Even as I pondered, the footsteps started again; someone in Mr. Waters's office was opening drawers and rummaging inside them, apparently searching for something. "I called out 'Who is there?' There was no answer. I called again, 'Who is in there?' but all was silent.

"After a few seconds the shuffling started again as before. Plainly the office was being searched for something urgently needed. More than a trifle uneasy I called out very loudly, 'Right, I have asked you before, who is in there? If this is a joke I fail to see it. Answer, damn you, you have no right in there.'"

By now LAC Joyce was out of bed - his heart raced faster as thoughts raced through his mind - he must answer now he thought. But once again the only response was a chilling, eerie silence.

Joyce had to act now and he slowly pulled his tunic on over his pyjamas. Picking up his keys he went into the hallway lit by the blue light. He tried the outer door - it was locked, as it should have been. He quivered. With a quick glance round he tried all the other doors - they were locked, as he knew they would be.

His hair stood up on the back of his neck as he put the key in Mr. Waters's office door, slowly opened it, felt for the switch and put the light on. There was no one in there.

"The only place a person could be concealed was behind three aircrew type steel lockers standing about eighteen inches from the far wall. I walked over and looked behind them. No one was there," said Joyce. "Then in a flash it happened. Someone moved swiftly behind me, walked over and switched the light off, hurried over the hallway, flung the outer door open and walked very quickly up the concrete path into the night. My hair stood on end and was still stiff upright as I switched the light on."

Joyce paused for quite a while - then, having plucked up courage, tried the outer door. It was locked. Joyce froze - he was all locked in the building - yet, someone had been in there with him.

He was dumfounded, dazed and very frightened. He did not know what to make of it and his first thought was to call in the old LDV guard but decided not to. He slowly made his way back to his room; but, before doing so, once again tried all the doors; they were locked and secure.

Still with his tunic over his pyjamas Joyce lay on his bed, his ears alert for the slightest sound. Nothing more happened, and at 4 a.m., Joyce was still wide-awake. Just in case there was more ghostly happenings he had left his light on, but there was only the eerie silence. Finally he managed to sleep; and slept for an hour or so and was mighty relieved to hear with the dawn the footsteps of the first armourer coming on duty. Saying nothing of the night's events he hastened to the billet for a cold bath and breakfast.

In the dining hall he met LAC Zeke Gamble and LAC Lofty Gould. At last Zeke said, "What's up with you Junker? You're quiet this morning. Has she ditched you, cocker?"

"No, nothing like that," replied 'Junker' Joyce and he then went on to explain what had happened in the night,

"Don't be daft, Junker," Zeke said. "You imagine things. There's no such things as ghosts, if that's what you think it was."

"Hold hard," said Lofty, "is that straight up, Junker?" Gripping Lofty's arm Joyce told him in no uncertain manner that he would hardly be likely to make it up.

Lofty was a photographer and he then told them something that made Zeke Gamble stop and think again. In charge of the Photographic Section was a Squadron Leader Goodhart. Late one evening quite recently, Goodhart was lying on his bed in the Officers Mess reading. Across the corridor from his room was the room of Squadron Leader Ingham, unoccupied since the Defiant crash in July. To his utter astonishment, Squadron Leader Goodhart heard Ingham's door open, and somebody walk down the corridor to the bathroom at the end, whistling just like Ingham used to do.

Goodhart leapt from his bed just in time to see Ingham walking down the corridor in shirt and slacks with a towel over his shoulder heading for the bathroom, which he entered. Goodhart followed him, opened the bathroom door and put the light on. There was no one in there.

Squadron Leader Goodhart had told Lofty never to tell anyone else what had been said, and as far as Lofty was concerned, the sooner forgotten the better. They changed the subject and tucked into their breakfasts.

A few days later, however, LAC Joyce was told to report to the Armoury Office and there he met Flying Officer Bibby, the Armament Officer, and Squadron Leader Goodhart, the officer in charge of the Photographic Section. LAC Joyce saluted.

"LAC Joyce," said Squadron Leader Goodhart. "Yes Sir," replied Joyce. Squadron Leader Goodhart was a New Zealander; and a gentleman of the old school and very much liked by the men. He asked about the ghostly affair of some nights ago and Joyce told him exactly what had happened.

Then to his surprise Squadron Leader Goodhart told him of his experience. Joyce stood and listened and was careful not to mention that he already knew. He asked Joyce what he made of it all and Joyce replied that he did not know. He did not like to mention Squadron Leader Ingham.

There was a knock on the door and in came Mr Frank Waters. "Perhaps," he said, "this might be of interest to you, gentlemen. It has been in my desk drawer for some time now."

He did not know that Squadron Leader Ingham previously occupied his office.

Mr. Waters handed a photograph to Squadron Leader Goodhart; who looked long and hard at the photograph; then handed it to LAC Joyce.

It was a picture of a very smart officer of the Royal Air Force, beside him stood a very beautiful lady, and hand of man and lady rested on the head of a tiny infant.

THE HAUNTED BOMBER

The Royal Air Force Museum at Cosford in Shropshire has its own resident ghost - called Fred. The ghost was first seen after the arrival of a Lincoln bomber, No. RF398, in 1977. The early post-war bomber was in need of repairs and one in charge was ex-RAF engineer John Small who had serviced Lincolns in the Middle and Far East. "The first time I saw the phantom airman I was speechless," said John. "He was sitting on a toolbox inside the Lincoln. Then he vanished."

Many of the volunteers working on the Lincoln have seen the phantom airman in blue battledress jacket and a white polo-neck sweater. Many people have heard footsteps coming along the fuselage only to turn and see no one there.

The ghost airman has been seen by many people in the Lincoln bomber; and in the hangar. Also, since the appearance of the phantom airman there has been some eerie goings on … Strange whistling of an unidentifiable tune has been heard many times in the museum; another time an engineer working on the Lincoln bomber fell backwards to the floor without hurting himself; and, during a very cold spell the aircraft interior was warm enough to work in without a jacket.

"It is all very eerie," said John Small, "so very puzzling, but everything that happens appears to be for the Lincoln bomber. The job of rewiring through the wings should have taken weeks but it was done in 48 hours."

One Sunday afternoon in September 1980, Mrs Greaves of Cannock, Staffordshire was visiting the Museum at Cosford. "It was about 4 p.m.," she said, "I looked up to the cockpit of the Lincoln bomber, and saw a figure of a fair-haired man in a white polo neck sweater, and wearing a forage cap. I felt very puzzled on seeing the figure and it bothered me for a day or two, because he was not in regulation uniform." Mrs Greaves added: "He appeared to be an officer to me, and I just felt he should not have been there in the cockpit."

There are one or two theories about the phantom airman. "One is that it could be a Spitfire pilot who was killed when his aircraft crashed," said Mr Small. "It was refurbished and put in the hangar. But it has gone, and the phantom airman is still here."

Another theory is that it is the ghost of an engineer; who killed himself, when the bomber he was responsible for crashed in the late 1940s killing all the crew. Some parts of the crashed bomber found their way into the hangar.

There have been other theories about the phantom airman being an engineer, for during the war, over 70,000 engine and airframe mechanics and armourers passed through Cosford. The station opened in 1938 and throughout the war years RAF Cosford housed No.9 Maintenance Unit in No. 41 Group. They handled many kinds of aircraft, but the main ones were Spitfires and Wellingtons.

Also, an RAF Military Hospital was established at Cosford during the war; and it became one of the best in the world with true RAF doctors and QA Nurses Second to none in the world. One of the top RAF Surgeons at RAF Military Hospital Cosford was Wing Commander Keir. Then Common Sense played a large part and one section was a large RAF Military Isolation Hospital.

So, there are many theories for the phantom airman. One thing is certain - he is at home in the old Lincoln bomber.

THE MAN WHO NEVER WAS

Two weeks after his 21st birthday David Petrie joined the Royal Air Force VR in July 1942. After a period in the Middle East, he returned to Blighty, and after a week's disembarkation leave, he was posted to RAF Manston in Kent.

RAF Manston was one of three Bomber Command Emergency Landing Grounds - the other two being Woodbridge in Suffolk and Carnaby in Yorkshire. All three were coastal airfields specially designed to handle crippled bombers in any kind of situation.

With the aid of FIDO, landings could be made in all weather conditions. Manston was also fully equipped with Emergency Services.

Sergeant David Petrie arrived at RAF Manston in April 1944 and; he was put in charge of a Crash Crew Section. It was a job that needed a lot of stomach, and within days, he was cutting out dead and wounded aircrew from shot-up bombers.

It was just after D-Day and Sergeant Petrie was again on duty. One morning just after 11 a.m. Manston received information that there was a crippled bomber limping home across the Channel and trying to make it to the emergency airfield.

The message was conveyed to the crash crew; and upon receipt of it, Sergeant Petrie and his crew raced down the special long runway to a point nearest to an estimated crash landing.

After a short wait a Lancaster bomber crash-landed with its port undercarriage damaged, consequently it skidded across the runway and caught in some wire netting with its starboard wing high in the air.

The port inner was feathered when it crashed and smoke was coming from the starboard outer engine.

The crippled bomber still had its full crew on board and as the aircraft screeched to a stop, the crew made a hurried exit; and in so doing, the pilot left the engine running. The crash crew were there by the time the bomber halted; and quickly sizing up the situation, Sergeant Petrie decided to eliminate any risk of fire and boarded the aircraft to switch the engine off.

On entering the aircraft he met a civilian wearing a brown pin-stripe suit; and told him that he had better get out quick, because of the risk of fire.

Sergeant Petrie gave him no more thought as he was having difficulty in trying to locate the switch.

"The next thing that I knew was that a man leaned across and switched the engine off," said Sergeant Petrie.

After making sure that everything was safe, Sergeant Petrie made his way out of the aircraft as quickly as possible; and, as he turned to walk away, saw an elderly RAF Sergeant standing near the door of the aircraft.

On seeing the Sergeant, Sergeant Petrie asked him if he could tell him where the civilian in the brown pin-stripe suit had gone, as he would like to thank him for perhaps saving his life.

"You must be seeing things," replied the Sergeant. "There are no civilians allowed on this airfield." Sergeant Petrie did not believe him - he had seen him, spoken to him; and as he was the only person in the aircraft with him, he had to be the person who switched off the engine.

Sergeant Petrie would not take no for an answer and throughout the day he persistently asked the other Sergeant about the civilian. He was repeatedly told:

"Forget it son - there was no one there other than the crew, only you came out of the Lancaster."

After eight months at RAF Manston, Sergeant Petrie was posted to No.2 Armoured Car Company, Aden, January 1945 to October 1946, from where he was demobbed.

Four decades later, former Sergeant Petrie is still adamant about the figure he saw in the crippled Lancaster bomber. "Someone switched off the engine and it was not me," he said. I am certain, that unbeknown to Sergeant Petrie, it was his Guardian Angel who switched off the engine.

THE GHOST OF RAF WITTERING

With the tide turning in favour of the Allies there was a build-up of aircraft on many airfields and soldiers were sent to guard them. Private Easters with the Leicestershire Regiment was detailed Aircraft Guard Duty. They were posted to RAF Wittering, which was a few miles south of Stamford, by the main A1 Road.

RAF Wittering was a First World War site, which was further developed during 1924; and opened as a Training Station with the Central Flying School. At the outbreak of the Second World War No. 11 Flying Training School replaced it; and the customary two Fighter Squadrons took up residence.

The airfield was too far north to become involved in the Battle of Britain, but it played a major part in the defence of the Midlands. For the next few years there were always three or more fighter squadrons in attendance and many enemy aircraft were destroyed.

During 1943 the station housed P38 Lightnings and PSI Mustangs of No. 55 Fighter Squadron USAAF. When the Air Fighting Development Unit arrived there were many types of aircraft; and in addition to the RAF, the Royal Navy was also attached with their Fulmar, Barracudas and Seafires.

One August night in 1944, Private Easters was on Guard Duty on 'D' Dispersal. It was about 8 p.m. and a beautiful clear evening. He was just enjoying a smoke after the NAAFI van had been.

"I know I should not have been smoking," he said. "Anyway, I was just taking a last drag of my cigarette, when suddenly I heard a swishing sound; like the sound of a shell going through the air. I looked up and saw this phantom bomber coming across the runway. It was only about 30 feet high and it headed straight towards the control tower."

Private Easters was rooted to the ground. He was puzzled because it made only a swishing sound, no engine noise, and even more bewildered when the phantom bomber just disappeared in front of his eyes. Later he learned, that a bomber returning from a bombing mission in the early days of the war, had crashed into the control tower. There were no survivors.

Flt Lt Devonshire

In the early 1970s Flight Lieutenant Len Devonshire was posted to RAF Wittering as an Air Traffic Controller. The station was now the home of the Harrier, with No.1 Squadron; and Hunters with Nos. 45 and 58 Squadrons. One November night Flight Lieutenant Devonshire was on duty in the control tower with a WAAF Duty Officer. She had just made them both a cup of coffee when suddenly they looked at each other in amazement as they heard footsteps coming up the stairs. For security reasons the door into the control tower and operations block are always locked. So, they were very alarmed to hear footsteps.

"She told me off for not locking the outside door properly," recalls Len Devonshire; "and we both went to the landing to see who it was who had got into the control tower building. A man in World War Two style flying suit, fur lined boots and leather helmet was coming up the stairs."

They both stood petrified - unable to speak and could not believe what they were seeing.

"He passed by us," said Len Devonshire, "he did not seem to see us and made no attempt to communicate. His footsteps echoed along the landing as the ghost flyer went into the Senior Air Traffic Controller's office. After a few minutes he came out of the office and went down the stairs again.

"The hair was standing up on the back of my neck; and, it was a reflex action because I certainly wasn't afraid. As a man of action, I should have done something. But, the incident was so unexpected, I was paralysed;" and he added: " He was as real and solid looking as anyone of us on duty at this moment."

After the departure of the ghost flyer they both sat down and discussed the incident. But before doing so they checked the outside door ... it was still securely locked.

They later learned that a crew returning from a wartime bombing mission had crashed into the control tower. There were no survivors. Was it the same aircraft that Private Easters had been told about? And was the ghost flyer from the phantom bomber seen by Private Easters?

"I'm sure that the ghost we both saw in the control tower was part of that crew," said Len Devonshire. "When we told our story, we heard of others who had seen the same figure in the control tower building; as if it were continually looking for something."

THE PHANTOM POLISH FLYER

In March 1945 'Grandad' Madison was digging out a deep ditch at the side of a farm track; when he glanced up and saw an airman in flying kit walking along the track towards him.

He did not think anything out of the ordinary on seeing the airman, for the farm he was working on was close to RAF Blyton in Lincolnshire.

RAF Blyton opened as a heavy bomber station in November 1942, and it housed No. 199 Squadron; but for some unknown reason, the role of the station changed, and for the duration of the war it housed No. 1662 Heavy Conversion Unit.

Bombers took off night and day and there were many crashes with Heavy Bombers strewn around in the fields close to the airfield. It was an airfield with a sad atmosphere, and it was disliked by almost everyone.

So, to 'Grandad' Madison it was not an uncommon sight to see an airman in full flying kit. Assuming he was a survivor, who had perhaps baled out from a crippled bomber, he shouted to the airman, "Do you need any help?"

The airman turned his head towards Mr. Madison and his mouth opened and shut as though speaking; but no sound was heard.

Thinking that the airman must be dazed and in shock, 'Grandad' climbed out of the ditch and on to the track. In doing so he ducked his head and lost sight of the airman for a few seconds, and when he stood up on the track the airman was nowhere to be seen.

Mr. Madison was very puzzled and he searched the ditches and fields close at hand, but could find no trace of the airman.

But now, Mr. Madison was quite disturbed, and he went to the farmhouse and told the farmer what he had seen. Mr. Madison was so adamant that he had seen an airman in full flying kit that the farmer contacted RAF Blyton, but they said that none of their aircraft were missing on that day.

However, an RAF officer came to see Mr. Maddison and he described the mystery flyer to him. But that was the last Mr. Madison heard about it, and he never saw the airman again.

In 1967 the remains of a bomber fuselage with its five Polish crew was recovered whilst dredging a deep wide drain between the farm and the River Trent.

The wings and tail had snapped off, the fuselage had sunk, and the water had continued to flow through the shattered fuselage for over twenty years, until the drain was dredged for the first time since the war.

At the inquest, a Polish ex-airman came from London and produced the Station Log Book for RAF Blyton. It showed that on a certain date this aircraft had taken off with five Polish airmen in it. Their bodies were later laid to rest in the Polish cemetery at Newark, Nottinghamshire.

It turned out that the track where 'Grandad' Maddison saw the mystery flyer was in a straight line between the point where the aircraft crashed and RAF Blyton. The phantom Polish airman was walking towards the aerodrome.

The old control tower standing in a derelict condition on the western side of the site at RAF *Blyton – an eerie silence and an even sadder atmosphere when the mist rolls in – it is hard to imagine that this was once the centre of a wartime airfield*

THE HAUNTED HANGER AT SOUTH CARLTON

During the very early days of the Second World War, Ron Lines and four comrades were posted to South Carlton, a small village just a few miles north of Lincoln, to form a workshop detachment for the service and repair of Army vehicles in that area. They were a small detachment from the Royal Army Service Corps and Ron Lines trade was an Electrical Artificer in Army workshops.

On arrival at South Carlton they found that their workshop and billet was an old First World War hangar, with a long winding drive bordered with rhododendron bushes winding out at the roadway.

South Carlton aerodrome was constructed between the Ermine Street and B1398 roads immediately to the north of Hallifirs Wood and it opened in November 1916.Throughout the war it housed training units with a variety of aeroplanes, and there were many fatal crashes.

The steep Lincoln Cliff was a favourite location with the planners of World War One aerodromes, for they could make use of the prevailing southwesterly wind.

South Carlton closed in 1920 and the site reverted to agriculture, after the Royal Air Force vacated it. The local farmer used many of the military buildings; but many were pulled down, including some of the seven permanent Bessaneaux hangars.

However, one hangar remained in fair condition at the start of the Second World War; and it was to this hangar, that Ron Lines and his comrades were posted.

On entering the hangar they found an area of about 90 square feet partitioned off in one comer, with corrugated sheeting about 20 feet high, which was to be their workshop. Another section became the stores, and finally a separate area was to be their sleeping quarters.

Soon after the five of them had settled in they realized that there was something strange about the hangar and the old derelict buildings of the old South Carlton aerodrome.

"Almost every time we returned to our billet after an evening out, we would hear footsteps on the gravel path as we approached the drive, followed by the sound of someone brushing past the bushes quite clearly," said Ron Lines.

This was experienced by all of them. At first they thought it was intruders or courting couples but after investigating they never found anyone.

As time went by they became convinced about the strangeness of the old World War One aerodrome. "The place was haunted and one night we had proof of this when I clearly saw a ghost," said Ron.

The entrance to their workshop was a small door let into the large sliding doors, which was kept locked when the men were absent or sleeping. There were also two large 'drop open' windows, which were about ten feet from the ground, and they were always kept closed.

There was a pedestrian door at the rear into the vast empty hangar, which was also kept locked.

Night after night as they lay in their beds they could all clearly hear footsteps on the concrete floor of the empty hangar. Each time they would get up to investigate; but they never found anyone.

"One night just after going to bed - the others had already dropped off to sleep - I heard the 'thumb latch' on the small door click several times," Ron Lines recalls. "I thought someone was trying to break in. I then heard the large sliding doors, as though being forced sideways, but I knew these were also locked. Then after a few seconds I heard one of the high windows drop open (bearing in mind these were over ten feet above the ground).

"I lay listening - there was an eerie silence, followed by a thud as if someone had jumped down into the workshop, then without hesitation the footsteps strode smartly - as you would hear on the parade ground - across the workshop to the billet door.

"A misty blurred figure walked smartly to the foot of the bed next to me and turned and looked straight down into the face of Jock who was sleeping there. I shouted 'Jock - put the light on quick.' We all sat up in bed but the apparition vanished."

Ron added: "It was my instant opinion that it was a military person, because of the 'smartness' of step, and smart about turn at the foot of the bed, remembering that the phantom figure actually walked past the head of Jock's bed as it came through the door."

GUARDIAN SPIRIT

Defiant Aircraft

Brice and Powell walked slowly from the Guardroom towards the top hangar on 'A' Site at RAF Brize Norton in Oxfordshire. It was 25 November 1941, and a cold, black morning.

The airfield had only been open a few years and it first housed No.2 Flying Training School. It remained a Flying Training Station after the outbreak of war, and it also housed No.6 Maintenance Unit (MU). This was a 41 Group Unit housed in the southeast corner of the airfield with a few buildings, which included Lamella hangars. These hangars were grass covered with no windows and it was to one of these hangars that Brice and Powell headed.

It was about 07.20 hours by the time they reached the hangar side door, unlocked it and stepped inside. Instantly both men felt as if they had stepped into another world and Brice was aware of a large beam of light, some four to six feet high where one would expect absolute blackness. It was uncanny but there was no feeling of fear. Within about ten seconds Powell had found the main switch - only a few yards from the door - and banged it on. Immediately he had done so all the hangar lights came on and on doing so the apparition disappeared. Powell called out "Did you see that ghost?" At that time Brice had been looking directly over a Defiant, the tail facing him for the hangar was full of Defiants - all sprayed black and many with patches over bullet holes.

The Boulton Paul Defiant had a single 1,030 h.p. Rolls-Royce Merlin engine with a crew of two and armament of 4 x 303-inch guns in a single power-operated, 4-gun turret on top of fuselage behind the pilot. They were used for night fighter patrols, and had a maximum speed of 300 m.p.h. at 17,000 feet with a service ceiling of 30,000 feet.

Brice was drawn like a magnet towards the aircraft over which had been the beam of light; and as an electrician by trade, made an immediate investigation to see if anything was switched on inside the aircraft - but found nothing. However, while checking the aircraft he got a warm feeling of protection; and even when he caught his hand in his hurry to checkout the aircraft, he had no cut or felt no pain.

He jumped from the wing and stared at the Defiant. The aircraft number was to be forever imprinted in his mind - it was N3312; and later, when he saw the aircraft being towed out of the hangar, he again got that warm feeling of confidence that the aircraft would be safe and protect its crew.

Whatever Brice saw early that November morning in 1941 we shall never know. However, what we do know is the fact that he was right about that feeling of protection. Defiant N3312 was delivered to the RAF at No.6 MU on 6 November 1940. On 23 November 1940, it was allocated to No. 255 Squadron, which had just formed at Kirton-in-Lindsey in Lincolnshire; to join the resident squadron and No: 71, the first American Eagle Squadron which had just arrived with Hurricane IIas Fighters. At this stage America was still officially neutral, but these brave young men had volunteered to join the Royal Air Force.

In the early days No: 255 Squadron also operated from RAF Hibaldstow and there were a great many accidents as the squadron took on a night fighter role with its Defiants.

After a few weeks with two non-flying units, Defiant N3312 returned to No.6 MU at Brize Norton, which was when Brice saw it. It then went to No. 256 Squadron, and on 4 May 1942 to No. 288 Squadron. It flew many night sorties and on 15 January 1943 it was involved in a slight accident, but the aircraft absorbed the impact and its crew came to no harm. They stepped safely from the crippled aircraft.

Defiant N3312 was repaired at No. 10 MU, but at some stage in this repair work it was converted to a target tug configuration and was not reallocated to a unit until 7 January 1945, when it went to RAF Worthy Down. (It was in store at No. 10 MU from February 1944 until allocation to Worthy Down.)

From Worthy Down it was returned to No. 10 MU on 16 April 1945 and was struck off charge on 14 November 1945. Its war days were over.

Defiant N3312 came through the war safely, having done battle in those dark early days of war, and protected those who flew in her.

Had Brice seen a Guardian Spirit over N3312 that cold dark morning in November 1941?

Yes, I am certain he saw the aircraft's Guardian Spirit; and those who took to the war torn sky in Defiant N3312 would certainly agree with me.

THE HAUNTED FLIGHT LINE

After spending five years in the Royal Air Force as an airframe fitter, Peter Hyde got a job with Airwork Services Ltd., servicing Canberras at RAF Bassingbourn in Cambridgeshire.

Bassingbourn was an old World War Two airfield that opened in March 1938. Wellington and Whitley bombers operated from Bassingbourn in the early days of the war. At the end of 1942 the Americans arrived with Boeing B-17 Flying Fortresses. These were the 91st Bomb Group and they flew many missions, including raids on Peenemünde and Schweinfurt.

After the war the Americans moved out and the RAF returned in June 1945. Post-war the station housed many units, and in 1950 the Americans returned and B-29 Superfortresses arrived at Bassingbourn; but their stay was short and they departed in September 1951.

The jet-age came to the station when Canberra Bombers arrived in February 1952. Canberras remained at Bassingbourn up until the airfield closed in 1969.

Peter Hyde was with No: 231 OCU; and worked on Canberra T.4s, B.2s and PR.3s, the latter whose flight line was on the old north side of the runway.

One night in October 1968 Peter Hyde was doing an 'After Flight (AF) Service' after night flying on a Canberra PR.3 which was parked on a lonely old World War Two dispersal pan. He asked one of the other fitters in the rear cockpit how long he would be, as he wanted to lock it up. But there was no one there.

"I realized I hadn't actually seen him but I felt him there in some way, said Peter; and he added: "I just knew someone was there. I had even dropped some banter to him when I was up in the driver's seat."

There was an eerie atmosphere on the dispersal pan as Peter Hyde locked up. He then hurried back to the line office with a funny feeling in the back of his neck.

About a year later Peter Hyde was on night flying on the Canberra T.4 flight. The PR Canberras had long since abandoned this old flight line and moved to the south side of the airfield. The ground crews were chatting in the crew room while the aircraft were flying and during conversation someone mentioned that the old PR line was supposed to be the haunt of some ghostly airman.

It was the first Peter Hyde had heard of it; and it brought back memories of the night he was talking to himself. On hearing that the old PR line was haunted, he thought he would try and find out more about it. Having nothing better to do he jumped into the half-ton truck which was outside the office, and drove over to the old flight line. The truck had a steel rear body cover, and with headlights full on he drove slowly round the old buildings and pans looking for anything unusual - nothing.

He came to the last pan and drove slowly round in a circle; he was just going round again when suddenly there were two loud thumps on the tin side of the truck. With that Peter put his foot hard down on the accelerator and raced back to his own end of the airfield.

Back at Base, and with a bit more sense, he checked the back of the truck to see what had fallen over and banged on the side - that had to be the answer, for he was slowly turning in a circle at the time; but on looking in the back he found the truck completely empty. What or who bashed the truck?

It could not have been anyone having a joke, for Peter drove in a complete circle, - his headlights full on, and there was no cover for anyone to hide. Had Peter Hyde found the ghost and were the two thumps on the truck side a signal to him - or were they a warning to go away?

"I don't know what made me go and look," said Peter, "I just had this feeling. I often wondered about ghosts and now I have seen, or rather felt, the presence of one."

THE GHOSTS OF GOXHILL

Goxhill control tower

Goxhill, the most northerly of the Lincolnshire sites, for it was almost on the desolate south bank of the Humber, and certainly one of the most isolated airfields. It was a place of mystery that records do not solve and the ghosts are there to guard their secret.

The airfield was never operational yet it had a decoy airfield at Burnham, a few miles to the west of the airfield.

It was a standard bomber station, with three concrete runways, the main one on an axis north-east, south-west. The technical site, two 'T2' and one 'J' type hangars were on the west side of the airfield close to the minor road. The control tower was sited just forward of the 'J' type hangar.

RAF Goxhill opened in June 1941 as a Bomber Airfield in No.1 Group, Bomber Command but received no bomber squadrons.

In December 1941 the airfield was transferred to No.12 Group Fighter Command and it became a fighter station in the Kirton-in-Lindsey Sector but for some unknown reason that was not to be.

The mystery of the former bomber station takes another turn in June 1942, when it became a station of the American 8th Air Force. This was very strange for Goxhill was a long way from their stamping ground, which was in East Anglia.

However, this was to be the role of the airfield, now Station 345, and it was to receive newly arrived Fighter Groups from the United States of America, which trained here to acclimatize themselves in English weather and operational techniques. There was also – this the first time told – a Top Secret (no records kept) American Special Unit that I mention in Ghost Stations™ The Story.

The first Americans to arrive were the USAAF 1st Fighter Group in June 1942 with P-38 Lightning aircraft; and by the end of 1943 the American build-up at Goxhill was complete. In December of that year, the 496th Fighter Training Group (FTG) was formed with two squadrons, the 554th specializing in training for the P-38 Lightning and the 555th which flew P-51

Mustangs. The training proceeded, and by the end of October 1944 there had been 118 accidents, with 53 aircraft lost, 23 pilots killed and seven injured.

After the war the airfield was transferred to RAF Fighter Command; and until it became inactivated in December 1953, the airfield was used for bomb storage.

In January 1962 the airfield and technical site buildings were sold to Mr. John Faulding; who had farmed the area, and built a bungalow on the site in the late 1950's. However, the three hangars were not included in the sale and were retained by the Ministry of Supply (later the Ministry of the Environment) and were used for storage of Green Goddess fire engines and other items.

Today, the runways remain intact along with the hangars, control tower and operations block that, sadly, never knew the meaning of the word.

Having said that, many people have felt a presence in the dilapidated control tower.

"I went into the old wartime control tower at Goxhill," said Bernard Halford, "the floors had rotted away and I certainly had a feeling that I was not alone." Mr. and Mrs. Jackson are very level-headed people, very down to earth and the furthest thing from their minds was ghosts when they visited Goxhill airfield in the Sixties.

"It was an experience we will never forget," said Mr. Jackson. "My wife, who said she had a feeling of being watched, had returned to the car. I took a last look around and coming over the airfield to the left of the control tower was an aircraft that I recognized as a Lockheed P38 Lightning. It was easy to identify with its twin fuselage. The aircraft made a left-hand sweep, keeping the hangar to its left and, by so doing; I had a very good view of the underside. Suddenly, it just vanished. One second it was there before my very eyes; the next it was gone. I did not know what to make of it at first. It was so very eerie. I must have stood staring into space for a few minutes before I came to my senses and, I was soon in the car and away. We have never been back."

Mr and Mrs Jackson both had an eerie experience but they are not alone. One person said he saw two airmen and as they got nearer he could see that they were Americans. As he watched, they both walked through the side of the 'J' type hangar.

Another person said that in some parts of the airfield it is very cold; as if standing inside a refrigerator.

For an airfield that never saw action, it has many ghosts. What secrets do the Ghosts of Goxhill hide?

THE GHOSTS OF RAF NEWTON

RAF Newton has a long and chequered history that explains why the old former Fighter Airfield is haunted. It is ironic that the only RAF airfield in Nottinghamshire, still in use as at the time I write, should be one with grass runways; but that is the case and Newton is the airfield ... complete with ghosts.

Newton does have a long association with flying, an airfield first being established here in 1936 and becoming operational in 1940.

In July 1941, the station was transferred from Bomber Command to Flying Training Command and became home for Polish crews at No16 (Polish) Service Flying Training School and, there were many accidents. Of the Polish airmen trained at Newton, 42 had won British decorations by the end of the war.

There are many units at RAF Newton, one being the HQ Air Cadets which, has direct control of the Central Gliding School, located at RAF Syerston that lies derelict a few mile to the north-east.

Alan Waddington is the editor of Air Cadet News and since August 1988, had been living in the Officers' Mess at RAF Newton.

In 1990 he experienced one of the ghosts at RAF Newton. "The impression, will, I believe, last for ever," he said. Alan Waddington had been watching television in one of the rooms in the East Wing of the Officers' Mess.

For those not familiar with a Royal Air Force Mess, they are in the main a large central building, comprising a main entrance with anteroom (a formal lounge), dining room, bars and Mess offices and stores linked by two corridors to the two storey accommodation areas; comprising bedrooms, suites (for senior officers) and bathroom facilities.

Alan Waddington takes up the story: "Two corridors linking the main central ground floor area to the two accommodation areas; normally had two external doors facing out towards the front of the Mess.

"But at RAF Newton, because of a Royal Visit in the 1950's, an extension had been built to the ante-room on the right hand side of the main entrance; and a similar extension had been made to the left hand side of the building to accommodate a Royal retiring room, now known as the Ladies Room.

"Indeed, the accommodation I occupied was on the ground floor, past the Ladies Room, and in the West Wing. To get there from the East Wing I had to go past the ante-room. The main entrance, the bar and Ladies Room.

"On the night in question, I had been watching some late night television in the East Wing and, at about 11.50 I turned the television off and went into the corridor leading to the main corridor. The Mess was almost totally dark by then and there were few lights on even in the main corridor into which I now turned. The anteroom was being prepared for redecoration and much of the furniture had been removed; some painters' trestles were in place.

"I passed the first corridor set of double doors to my left and, as I came to the second set, which now led into the ante-room extension, I looked left, twice, in quick succession. For there at one side of the anteroom and, near where the original windows must have been, was a blue shimmering figure … hunched as if it were strapped to a parachute. I froze for a second.

" I could not believe my eyes, but there it was … and I walked on to the next main door and looked in on a totally darkened room with no sign of any person let alone a shimmering figure.

"I quickly walked to my room and went to bed wondering what I had seen; or was it some trick of the light or imagination; but then I had felt the hair at the back of my neck rise! And so it happened again when some days later I told my story to some of the Mess staff and other colleagues.

"Some days later I retraced my steps again in the late evening and confirmed that in no way could it have been my reflection in the glass door. However I was later told by one of the stewardesses on duty in the Mess that a "newly arrived" young steward had felt a "cold" sensation when he had been in the ante room. Where was he standing, I asked? When I was told, it turned out he had almost been on the spot where I had seen my shimmering airman!"

But Alan Waddington is not the only one to have had a ghostly experience at RAF Newton; for there have been many ghostly happenings.

One steward claimed that as he had been turning off the lights in the rooms and particularly in the main corridor between the East and West Wings; they were mysteriously turning on again behind him. Yet there was no one to be seen!

Another haunted area in the Mess is the shelter that is underground and a reminder of those wartime days. And when the door is opened into the main corridor it exudes damp, musty smell. Needless to say it is not often opened. However, the light that illuminates this damp musty stairwell with its gaudy mural, does appear to switch itself on without reason, yet nobody has any reason to go down there.

Or do they? The stewards say that when they had switched the Shelter light off; it suddenly came on again and they could not explain why that was so.

The answer for some of the ghostly happenings could stem from a former wartime Mess manager; who hanged himself in the Mess flat; which at that period was used as staff rest rooms.

Some say it is the ghost of the former wartime Mess manager taking his revenge.

However, the ghostly happenings are not only in the Mess building. In one of the former wartime hangars, that is now used as Motor Transport (MT) storage there are many strange happenings.

Airmen on night duty in the MT hangar find that all is peaceful and quiet; until they enter the Duty Room. Then the ghosts go to work.

Many on night duty have reported hearing doors opening; yet they are locked and the place is deserted. Or is it? No, certainly not, for the ghosts are restless.

At RAF Newton; doors move, locked doors open by a ghostly hand, stairs creak, lights mysteriously switch on and off and floorboards move … seemingly without explanation.

Air Display at RAF Newton in the Good Old Days

THE MYSTERIOUS MUSIC AT BAWDSEY MANOR

One of the most secretive places during the Second World War was RAF Bawdsey in Suffolk; and it holds many dark secrets that go way back. So first, let us look at the history of Bawdsey Manor, which has a most bewitching and interesting history.

Bawdsey Manor, perched on its Suffolk cliff top over-looking the sea and the mouth of the River Deben, is an impressive property with its cupola towers and turrets in a mixture of styles. The interior is as complicated as the exterior and equally reflects its whimsical development.

William Cuthbert Quilter built Bawdsey Manor, over a period of almost twenty years and, the end result proves that he had no idea what he was doing. Having said that; it was obviously what he was happy with; and that is all that matters. Work on Bawdsey Manor started in 1886 with no expense spared. It started life as a holiday home but, for some reason, the Quilter family decided to make the Manor their family home.

Why did Sir Cuthbert Quilter make his home Bawdsey Manor?

In 1883 Quilter had purchased the territorial 'Lords of the Manor' at Bawdsey and gradually acquired more land until he had an estate of 8,000 acres. Also in 1883 he rented Hintlesham Hall from the Anstruther family and kept it on for ten years.

As soon as it had been decided that the Manor would be the family home, the massive Red Tower was added in 1895. This provides the principal accommodation. Then came the white stone courtyard facade and the main entrance; the original front door is now somewhere inside the building. This facade was to provide the link with the White Tower that was completed in about 1905. Thus Bawdsey Manor was built in five stages over some twenty years.

Quilter was born in London in 1841. He was educated privately and at the age of 17 joined his father's accountancy firm. At 22 he became a stockbroker and was involved in a wide variety of financial enterprises. At his death in 1911 he left just short of £1,250,000. He retained till his death a large London home in Mayfair. He passed away at Bawdsey and was laid to rest in the family vault in the village.

The Air Ministry purchased Bawdsey Manor and grounds from the second Sir Cuthbert for £24,000 in 1936 and, a team of scientists moved in to work on RADAR.

The Radar Station was handed over to the RAF in May 1937 but scientists continued to develop it into the most comprehensive Radar Station. The Manor sprouted a mass of radar transmitter masts and, the 25 Radar Stations played a vital role in the early war years; all due to work done at Bawdsey Manor.

After the war, Bawdsey Manor remained a Radar Station and, also a training school until 1974. It was then reduced to care and maintenance with one resident caretaker, an RAF Sergeant, until re-opening in July 1979 when the Bloodhound Missiles from RAF Wittering, were deployed at Bawdsey Manor as part of the defence of RAF Wattisham.

Bawdsey Manor was also the home of an RAF Bomb Disposal Unit, which was in keeping with the Quilter family … I will explain in a moment.

"I took over command of RAF Bawdsey in January 1985 and remained in post until I had the sad task of closing it down on March 31, 1991," said Squadron Leader Derek Rothery.

The only reminders now of the early radar days are the porch floor which, contains a mosaic in the form of a dog on a chain, being a very close replica to the 'Beware of the Dog' emblem, a common Roman anti-burglar warning, the badge subsequently being adopted as the RAF Squadron's Official badge; and the number 2 tower which is used as a ship-to-shore radio link by Trinity House and the Felixstowe and Harwich Harbour Boards.

Also, one or two of the Chain Home transmitter and receiver buildings are still there. These are of brick within a blast wall.

During the war years and again during the 1950's, when Bawdsey was a fully Operational Radar Station, many airmen and other staff said they often heard piano music; playing the tune of Colonel Bogie. (many readers will remember the music from the film 'The Bridge on the River Kwai')

"I heard a piano being played many times," said one radar mechanic. It was Colonel Bogie. At first I never gave it a thought; you just heard it. Then I thought, there is no damn piano. But it was not frightening, quite the opposite. On hearing it you felt proud to be at Bawdsey. It gave you a proud sort of belonging feeling."

And he added. "Now that you ask and, I think about it, I always heard it when a bit down but, on hearing Colonel Bogie being played it made you forget the down side."

I can solve the mysterious music at Bawdsey Manor. Let me explain. Roger Quilter the composer (1877 - 1953) was Sir Cuthbert's third son.

Sir Raymond Quilter, the third baronet (1902 - 1959) was Sir Cuthbert's grandson. He was co-founder in 1932, with James Gregory, of the G.Q. Parachute Company. Sir Raymond was a leading parachute expert who made many descents himself. He flew his own aircraft from a private airfield on the estate.

And the connection with the Quilter family and RAF Bomb Disposal Unit which, I said I would explain. Sir Raymond's hobby during the Second World War was bomb disposal. He produced a special key for extracting fuses from enemy bombs.

That has solved the bomb disposal mystery; or should I say, explained that?

So now let me solve the mystery music and, to do so, I call upon Beryl Christiansen, whose mother worked at Bawdsey Manor in its heyday and, as her **exclusive** story unfolds, all will be made clear.

"My mother worked there," said Beryl Christiansen; "and she told me many stories about her life while living in this beautiful place.

"She paid 'half a crown', to obtain the position children's nurse to Miss Zoë & Miss Sonia Quilter. Sir Cuthbert & Lady Quilter were her employers and were lovely people to work for.

"They employed a tremendous staff, a butler, cooks, upstairs and downstairs maids, a nanny, stable boy, groom and several gardeners. My mother was about nineteen years old when she was hired to help 'Nanny' with the children.

"Every evening at 6.30 pm, Lady Quilter would go to the Nursery to see Miss Zoë and Miss Sonia. They would march round the room, while Lady Quilter played the 'Colonel Bogie March', and other resounding tunes on the piano!

"One evening she came earlier than usual. Nanny, my mother and the children, always ate tea in the Nursery... never with the family. It was customary for any employee to stand up out of respect, when Lady Quilter entered the room. Nanny took the comer of the tablecloth and quickly wiped her mouth, instead of using her napkin! That incident cost her 'instant dismissal'.

"She had been there for several years, - but indiscreet table manners in front of the children would not be tolerated, she found out. The poor Nanny was upset, but left that day and was not re-hired there.

"Every Christmas eve, Sir Cuthbert and Lady Quilter gave a magnificent Ball for the staff, this was held in the Ballroom, and was the highlight of the year for the employees. When the Butler asked my mother for a Waltz, she was absolutely thrilled, as the Butler was quite high up, and usually feared by all.

"Bawdsey Manor was the family's summer home. Their winter residence was Nethersgate Hall, Woodbridge I believe. I have been trying to find out more about this -stately home - but no one seems to know anything about it, or have even heard of its existence. Perhaps you could help me on this?

"Sir Cuthbert's brother, was Sir Roger Quilter, and he was a famous composer. I can remember as a child, listening to our old Echo wireless (radio), and my mother telling me, 'The Overture being played, is by Sir Roger Quilter' … so they were quite a famous family.

"My mother's maiden name was Ethel Dennant. She married my father, Frederick Rowland in 1920. Both are dead now, but if my mother were alive today, she would be so excited about you writing memories of beautiful Bawdsey Manor. She often used to tell me: 'that living there, was like living with Royalty' and those days were some of the happiest memories in her life."

And for all those who heard the mysterious music ... Colonel Bogie ... it brought them a sense of happiness.

So was the music a means of making those who worked at Bawdsey Manor, content in their duties?

It certainly seems so.

The Station badge of RAF *Bawdsey. In the floor of the entrance porch is a mosaic, an almost exact copy of a 'Beware of the Dog' emblem, a common Roman anti-burglar warning. One can today, see one in the entrance of a house in Pompeii and, one in Naples Museum. The one at Bawdsey Manor was bought from Italian craftsmen when Quilter took his steam-yacht Peridot through the Mediterranean to the Aegean. This watchdog, as you can see, was adopted as the unit's official badge, which was very fitting, for it symbolised the unit's role as part of the air defence of the United Kingdom.*

It is interesting to note that during the war years, Lord and Lady Quilter used to deliver the milk; and the RAF who served at Bawdsey had a strange custom which, it seems, was in keeping in Bawdsey's tradition of strangeness.

Adjoining the Leather Room that was Quilter's study, features carved oak panelling throughout with embossed leather (completely replaced in 1986) and, Victorian fireplace with ornate carved surround with ten coats of arms, is the bar - conservatory with three-panelled fireplace. Each panel has a date-digit in the diamond. It is said that the original second panel is the missing one and that the full date should read 1674 or even 1574.

Footprints on the ceiling, directly in front of the bar, were part of RAF Bawdsey tradition. When an officer or SNCO was posted, they left their mark.

And I can reveal, there **is** a secret door.

And black swans lived on the Manor lake. Tunnels and grottoes link the gardens.

This, then, is Bawdsey Manor and its surrounding estate ... Outrageous style of cupola towers and turrets.

The birthplace of radar where hush-hush work was carried out by a team headed by the Scottish physicist Sir Watson-Watt. Strange traditions. Secret doors. Black swans and mysterious music. That is Bawdsey Manor that started life as a holiday home for Victorian magnate Sir Cuthbert Quilter.

Today, as I write (October 1993), Bawdsey Manor is a Grade 2 listed building and is offered for sale with 13 cottages and a sailing club, office blocks, extensive outbuildings, recreational facilities, gardens (where Percy Thrower's father worked) parkland and 150 acres of land.

There is much to remember Bawdsey Manor for; an interesting insight into Family life via my exclusive interview with Beryl Christiansen; the mysterious Colonel Bogie tune played on a piano and, happy memories for all who have served at Bawdsey Manor, good fortune has prevailed.

As stated, Percy Thrower's father was at Bawdsey Manor and Percy went on to television fame and fortune.

Sir Cuthbert Quilter's sister married into the famous Eley Cartridge family.

Sir Cuthbert was founder of real ale. He was a Member of Parliament (until 1906) and he rarely spoke in the house; but when he did it was about the need for pure ale. He felt so strong about it he bought Melton Brewery (now the Coach and Horses) and brewed real ale.

Radar was developed at Bawdsey Manor and, with that and the best fighter pilots in the world; we won the Battle of Britain.

So good fortune is Bawdsey Manor and, of course, the tune of Colonel Bogie.

… Are you whistling?

THE M11 PHANTOM FIGHTER

P-51 Mustangs

One night in March 1984, Paul Dixon set out from Sheerness in Kent to return home to Grimsby. It was just before midnight when he cleared Sheerness and headed towards London. About a mile or so ahead of Paul Dixon's lorry was his colleague who, had started out ahead of him. Both were heading north, both drivers being employed by the same shipping company.

It was an uneventful journey to London and soon they were on the M11 Motorway and heading north, homeward bound.

Paul Dixon, then aged 21, loved driving and was a cool-headed down to earth young man, not one to let his mind wander when behind the wheel, of his lorry ... his pride and joy.

Soon they were passing Junction 8 and Stanstead Airport. The two lorries headed north and it was a quiet run to Junction 9, the turning for Newmarket that stretch of the M11 Motorway, being the longest and most desolate. Up to that point, nothing out of the ordinary had happened; but that was soon to change.

It was only a short run from Junction 9 to Junction 10 and as they neared Junction 10 it was to be a journey they will never forget. Paul Dixon takes up the story:

"I was travelling north along the M11 in convoy with another driver called Brian who, was from Leeds. We were talking to each other via the CB radio; Brian was about half-a-mile in front of me.

"The night was cold but not frosty cold. Approximately half-a-mile from Junction 10, north bound, something black flew east-to-west, approximately one hundred yards in front of me. Closely followed by a pressure wave equivalent to a large lorry passing at speed.

"My own vehicle rocked about and I immediately pulled over on to the hard-shoulder, thinking that I had hit something. I contacted Brian by CB radio and told him that I had stopped. He came back on the air to say he would also stop and wait for me.

"I jumped out and checked over my truck with a torch. No damage … No blood … No scratches; there was nothing.

"I then realised I was stood on the motorway hard shoulder, at 1.30 in the morning; with no reason for being there and, no excuse for the police if they came.

"I carried on and caught Brian up. I told him via the CB what had happened and he laughed and, said words to the effect that I was a nutter and I had imagined it.

"Maybe so. I feel I am pretty level headed, intelligent and sober." And he added:

"For the record, I found out later that Junction 10 on the M11 is home to the Imperial War Museum at Duxford. Was it a lost soul returning home? Or was it my imagination? People I have related this story to have either laughed or shrugged their shoulders with indifference."

Was it Paul Dixon's imagination?

If it was his imagination then how do you account for the fact that I have three others on file who, have each experienced a similar encounter with the unexplained. All have had their vehicles violently rocked and were adamant that it had been caused by a low flying aircraft; but no one claimed to have heard it.

Bill Smith from Doncaster was returning home along the M11 Motorway after a weekend in Calais, in February 1993.

"I was about midway between Junctions 9 and 10 on the M11, when suddenly a dark shape passed very low over my car, causing it to rock, as if hit by a slip-stream," he said.

When asked to describe what he saw, Bill Smith replied: "Very difficult to say. I took it to be an aeroplane flying low because of the way it rocked my car. But on thinking about it, there were no lights and I never heard it.

Was it a UFO? Or was it something from the supernatural world?

All incidents took place between Junctions 9 and 10 on the M11 Motorway north and south-bound. And all were between 0100 and 0200 hours. Paul Dixon asked if it was a lost soul returning home to Duxford. It could well be, for RAF Duxford has a long history and, dates back to 1919. RAF Duxford housed a variety of squadrons and aircraft from early Gloster Gauntlets, to Blenheims, Spitfires and Typhoons to name but a few.

During the latter war years RAF Duxford housed the Americans with their P-38 Lightnings, P-39's and P-51 Mustangs; and history has proved it became one of the greatest piston-engine fighters of the Second World War. With a speed of 440mph and a range of 2,300, with external fuel tanks, it could escort bombers all the way to Berlin and back.

In the summer of 1968, RAF Duxford became the main base for the filming of the Battle of Britain. Today, it is the home of the Imperial War Museum, which took over from the East Anglian Aviation Society that had been formed by a group of very dedicated enthusiasts in order to save RAF Duxford.

From my research I have ascertained that the ghost flyer in his phantom aircraft, always makes his ghostly landing over the M11 Motorway to runway 06/24; and, it does look as if he is coming in to land at Duxford.

However, be that as it may, one must look at the old airfield at Fowlmere for the answer. This airfield was in very close proximity to Duxford.

Fowlmere opened in June 1940 as a satellite for nearby Duxford but it soon became an airfield in its own right. In 1943, the airfield, sited just south of Manor Farm was extended and, became Station 378 USAAF.

The Americans arrived with P-51 Mustangs and remained at Fowlmere until October 1945. During their stay, the 339th Fighter Group gave fighter cover for both heavy and medium bombers.

They also gave air cover over the Normandy beaches and during the battle of the Ardennes Sector in December 1944 and January 1945. I am certain that it is here is my answer for the phantom flyer; for on one of these raids, one veteran American pilot … who always said he would return - and by the crews considered a 'Good Luck Charm' for he always did return - was missing. To add to the mystery, his aircraft has never been found. That would explain the ghostly shadow of an aircraft as it made it back to base The young American pilot promised that he would return to Station 378 and that he is doing until set to rest.

Today, the old airfield at Fowlmere has gone, only a few decaying huts on the west side of Fowlmere village remains, otherwise, no trace to show that this was once an operational fighter airfield. Only the ghost flyer remains as he keeps his promise to return to base.

THE PHANTOM BED-CHECKER OF RAF HEREFORD

Each month, on average, I receive about a hundred letters, many with interesting stories and, one such letter was from Jan Thorpe who, encountered some ghostly experiences after she joined the Women's Royal Air Force, the WRAF for short. It all started after she arrived at RAF Hereford for her basic training at the WRAF School of Recruit Training. She ... better still, I will let Jan tell you in her own words about the Phantom Bed-Checker of RAF Hereford:

"After having first read two of your Ghost Stations™ books, two and four, I felt compelled to write and tell you of my ghostly experiences in the RAF.

"I joined the WRAF in January 1979 and went to RAF Hereford for my basic recruit, training and was billeted in Learoyd Block.

"Every evening we were bed-checked at midnight, I think it was. This meant that we all had to be in bed with lights out at this time and, we were checked by the Duty NCO who would walk down the full length of the room making sure we were all in.

"The room was occupied by either twelve or fourteen girls, so was quite long. This one particular night the Duty NCO was a few minutes early; but as we were all in bed in the dark, we thought no more about it. Until, that is, we were bed-checked again at midnight.

"As I was room leader, I asked the Duty NCO why we were being bed-checked again, was something wrong? She said that this was the first time she had been in and, what was I talking about?

"There was no way that our 'Phantom Bed-checker' was one of the girls playing tricks; as it definitely had metal segs in the shoes and we weren't allowed them until we were due to pass out. Everyone in the room heard it."

If recruit Jan Thorpe had read Ghost Stations™, the first volume, and the story about The Jilted Ghost, she might have had cause to be frightened by the presence of the Phantom Bed-Checker … But now that is gone, for in September 1982; the WRAF School of Recruit Training was transferred – due to cost cutting and a big mistake - from RAF Hereford, to form a joint School of Recruit Training at RAF Swinderby in Lincolnshire ... and there, they have their own ghosts.

THE LOCH NESS GHOST

Loch Ness, the home of 'Nessie' the Monster and, a ghost World War Two flier, is one of the largest freshwater lochs in Scotland.

'Loch Ness Monster is Nazi U-Boat' - screamed the full front-page of the Sunday Sport, Sunday, October 15, 1989. And, to support their claim, a photograph of a U-Boat, that was said to have been taken two weeks earlier by an American tourist.

The German U-Boat was quickly linked to Rudolf Hess, the deputy Fuhrer; and stories flowed like tales from the Arabian Nights, with as much credibility.

The German U-Boat in Loch Ness? This is Fiction. But what about the Loch Ness Monster … is that Fact or Fiction? And what about the Phantom flier? How does the phantom Second World War flier tie-in with Loch Ness and the Monster? Are they just stories created by people wanting publicity?

So let us look at the facts that we have on record. With the facts and two pennyworth of common sense we can soon solve it. The sightings of the Monster started in earnest during the 1930s and, one eye-witness account described the Monster as having a snake-like neck and head and was some fifty feet in overall length.

Over the years there have been many sightings, the sharp increase being due to the fact that communications across the Highlands of Scotland have improved, thus news of any sightings travels faster. Also, there is now a road by the loch-side; and coupled with all that there is greater public awareness. Monster hunters have been out in force; but there is no firm proof of 'Nessie'.

One expert said the Loch Ness Monster is nothing more than mass-hallucination. That I do not believe. And the noted anthropologist, Sir Arthur Keith, commented that the Loch Ness Monster was not a problem for zoologists but for psychologists. That also I do not believe; and for one to say they need to see a Trick Cyclist proves that they are two biscuits short of a picnic.

But that is only their opinion; and they do not have any proof to say that 'Nessie' does NOT exist. The Monster Legend has been around a long-long- time; and goes back into the mists of time.

In AD550 Saint Adamnan wrote about the Life of Saint Columba and, in his work he vividly describes the rescue of the Pict named Lugne from the attack of a Monster in Loch Ness. At the sight of the Monster, Saint Columba made the sign of the Cross in front of it and commanded it in the name of God to return to the deep. The Monster slipped beneath the waters, to the utter amazement of the Picts and, from that moment on they were converted to Christianity.

Picts by the way, were people older than the Gaelic and Brythonic peoples who once occupied Britain; and about the 9th century became finally amalgamated with the Scots … bringing with them the Legend of the Loch Ness Monster.

So does the Loch Ness Monster exist? It does according to Hector Boece, who in 1527 recorded in his book Scotorum Historiae - the History of Scotland, an account of a 'terrible beast,' as told by Duncan Campbell who saw the Monster climb out of Loch Ness and kill three men.

So an eye-witness account … and recorded. How many other sightings that were NOT recorded. Remember, at this period, Loch Ness was very inaccessible and travel was very difficult, not like it is today.

Further evidence to support that a Monster was lurking in Loch Ness, came from the Duke of Portland, who wrote to The Times in the 1930's, to say that in 1895, the forester, local hotel keeper and fishing guides, spoke often of the Loch Ness Monster. So is there a Monster Sea Serpent?

"I was at the Loch early one morning, at the crack of dawn, camera at the ready;" said Pete Smithson, "Suddenly I saw this figure coming, weaving like, towards me. I thought he had been in some sort of accident. I then saw he was dressed in wartime flying clothes, complete with parachute and harness.

"As he sort of staggered towards me I suddenly felt cold. By now he was no more than 10 to 15 feet away and I could clearly see his RAF uniform. I shouted: 'Are you alright?' At that point he arched his right-hand and pointed towards the Loch.

"I instinctively turned and looked out over Loch Ness in the direction in which he was pointing. I fully expected to see the Monster. I then had a funny feeling … the coldness had gone and, quickly turning to the stranger shouted, 'What is it?' … But he had vanished. I then realized it had been a ghost airman. But he looked so real. The only thing about him was he looked injured and his face was greyish.

"What a damn fool I felt, confronted by a ghost with my camera around my neck, yet I never had an inkling to take a photo."

That sighting was in September 1978 and since then, two other people have also informed me that they had seen a figure of an airman near Loch Ness that had vanished when near the Loch. They both said the figure had on parachute and harness.

So, what is the connection with the phantom airman? It is true that a Vickers twin-engined Wellington, N2980 R-Robert, crashed into Loch Ness on New Year's Eve, 1940. Caught in a snow storm one engine cut out and, unable to maintain height, the pilot, Squadron Leader Marwood-Elton, ordered the crew to bale out. They did so but, the rear-gunner's parachute failed to open properly and he was killed.

The Wellington bomber crashed in Loch Ness, the pilot and co-pilot having remained at the controls to keep the bomber steady while the crew made good their escape. They were unaware that the rear-gunner had been killed. Before the bomber sank into the Loch, they managed to scramble into the dinghy and, reach the safety of the shore.

So was it the air-gunner trying to give some sort of warning to the pilot? It is strange that the sightings of the phantom World War Two flyer, only started in 1978; a year after Robin Holmes of Heriot-Watt University, Edinburgh; located the wartime bomber.

For 37 years Wellington N2980, R - Robert, had remained undisturbed. Now, the bounty hunters were in full cry, for out of the 11,461 Wellingtons built, this was the only survivor. Yes, there had been hundreds, Germany had not destroyed them; but, after the war they were not wanted and melted down. No one was interested ... now everybody was interested.

In September 1988 they started to lift R-Robert from its last resting place; and all was going well, when suddenly, something gave – as if a warning to stop – and the bomber sank back into the Loch. That was that a sign to call a stop. Leave the Wellington bomber in peace; and that was what the phantom flyer was trying to say. That I am certain.

But they did not stop and after another attempt the Wellington bomber was brought out of the Loch. The tyres were still inflated and when a battery was put on, the navigation lights worked at once.

Wellington N2980, R – Robert was taken to the Brooklands Museum to be restored. But what about the Phantom World War Two flyer? Is he at peace now his bomber has been removed from its last resting place? Obviously not.

THE HAUNTED PAINTING OF DOUGLAS BADER

Group of 242 Squadron Battle of Britain Pilots. Squadron Leader Douglas Bader 4th from right (as looking at photo) Hurricane aircraft in background.

A haunted painting? Yes, haunted. The painting of Douglas Bader that hangs in the main dining-room (see map) at RAF Cranwell in Lincolnshire is haunted. This painting is very popular at Cranwell and new people are shown it on their first visit to the station. Unfortunately, not many people know about the background of the painting or of the ghostly face that appears, always in the same place, just to the right of Group Captain Douglas Bader's face, for there are no records available until now that is and, told here in Ghost Stations™ 4 for the very first time.

So, in my photographs, let us take a closer look at the haunted painting in which the ghostly face can be clearly seen; and as the story unfolds, you will see I have solved the mystery of the haunted painting. Even the most sceptical will have to accept that the picture of Group Captain Douglas Bader is haunted.

Aerial view of College Hall, Cranwell, with its Italianate domed tower and haunted painting in the dining room.

RAF Cranwell is a very old airfield. It lies just north-west of Sleaford between the A1 and B1429 roads, just west of the village of Cranwell and goes back as far as 1915.

The station opened in April 1916 as a Royal Navy Training Establishment, HMS Daedalus, to train officers and ratings of the Royal Navy on aeroplanes, kite balloons and dirigibles.

When the Royal Air Force was formed in April 1918 it took over Cranwell and there were many changes. It officially opened as a Cadet College on February 5, 1920, and has been in that role ever since.

In the 1930's the old wooden huts were replaced and the new college structure was formally opened in October 1934. The old wooden hangars were replaced by two 'C' type hangars that are the ones still in use today.

Training at Cranwell continued unabated between the wars but during this period only pilots were trained here and, a wide variety of aircraft flew from the two airfields. Many well-known personalities graduated from the college, including Group Captain Douglas Bader in 1930. The same Douglas Bader whose picture now hangs in the main dining room and is haunted by a ghostly face.

During the Second World War the majority of aircrew trained at Cranwell were from Commonwealth and Allied countries including, Free France, Belgium, Ceylon, Czechoslovakia and Turkey.

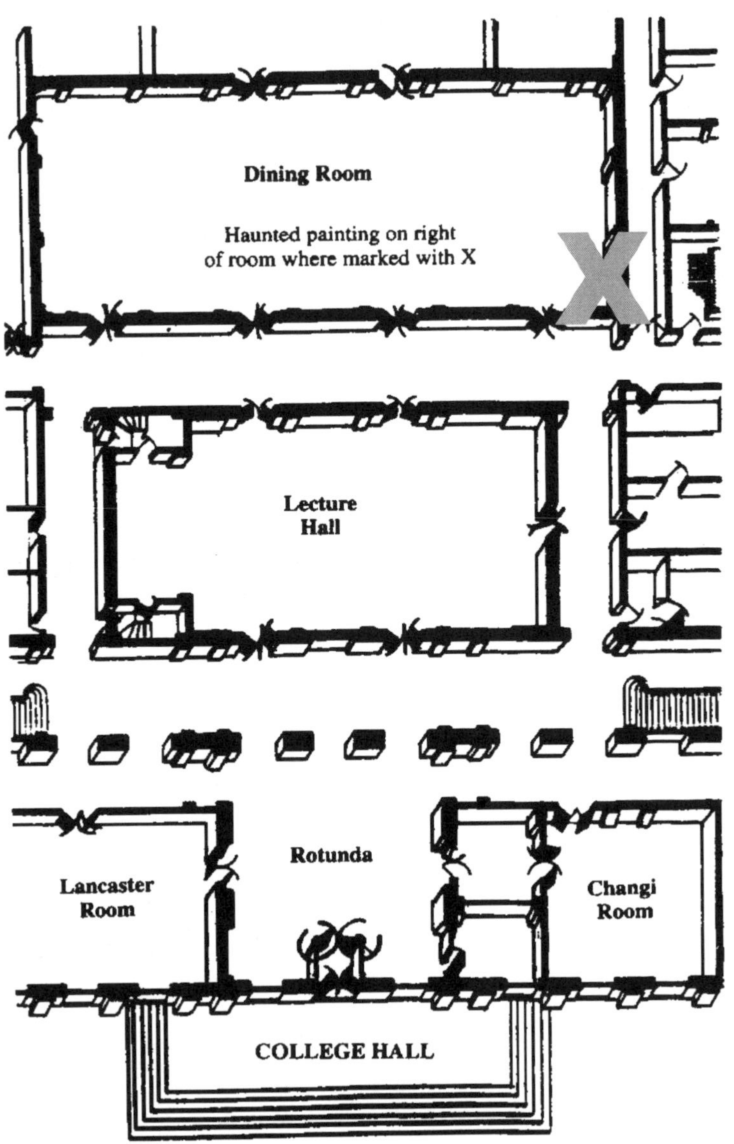

Section plan of College Hall, Cranwell, showing the dining room and where the haunted painting of Douglas Bader is located.

In the post-war years there were many changes. The evolution of the training had continued over the years and the aircraft were numerous, from the post-war Tiger Moths to the Tucano of today. Cranwell is constantly changing to keep its place as the RAF's number one college; and it is also number one of uncanny mysteries with having the haunted painting of Group Captain Douglas Bader.

One who has seen the ghostly face on the Bader painting is Lee Hatfield. He joined the RAF in 1985 and passed out in May of that year. In June he was posted to the RAF School of Catering at Aldershot and he arrived at RAF Cranwell at the end of July.

During his period at Cranwell, Senior Aircraftman Lee Hatfield's duties were those of Steward; thus, in that role, he had contact with the haunted painting. He has seen the ghostly face on the painting many times; as he now explains to my readers of Ghost Stations™4 …

"I have seen the face on the picture and I believe that it is what it is. I have no reason to doubt it but it's one of life's mysteries."

An eye-witness account proves it is not a trick. And my photographs of the haunted painting clearly shows not a trick of light or the imagination, for the ghostly face can be clearly seen and, it is not from the flash of the camera.

The two photographs (pages 183 and 184) taken close-up and each at a slightly different angle to show that it is not the flash.

The haunted painting of Group Captain Douglas Bader that hangs on the wall in the main dining room. If you look closely to the right of Bader's face, you will just see the ghostly face near the frame. This very clear on the following pictures.

On the top picture you can clearly see the ghostly face, which I have had ringed with a white circle, on just this photograph, so that you can clearly identify where on the painting the face appears … it is not the photoflash, as this is on the right arm on the picture above. The strip blur on the top of the painting is the orange picture light.

On the picture on page 184, again clearly seen the ghostly face, at the picture frame far right and level with Douglas Bader's face … right side. The photoflash is just off-centre of the painting, just below the chest on the right side.

And closer. The ghostly face clearly seen in the same position at the right of Bader's face. The photo-flash centre on painting.

And closer still … still the ghostly face can be clearly seen which is proof that the painting is haunted by the ghostly image.

And now just a view of the image, which is clearly a mysterious face.

So let us now look at the history of the painting. Shell Petroleum presented the painting of Group Captain Douglas Bader to RAF College Cranwell in 1947. Did they part with it because it was haunted?

Captain Cuthbert Julian Orde who was born on December 18, 1888 at Great Yarmouth, Norfolk, painted the painting of Bader. Orde, the son of Sir Julian Orde, joined the Royal Flying Club and he took his flying certificate on a Maurice Farman biplane at Brooklands in May 1916. At the end of the First World War Orde held the rank of temporary major.

During the Second World War Captain Orde served as a war artist and he drew pictures of the pilots of Fighter Command who, knew Orde as either 'Turps' or 'The Captain.'

Orde lived with the fighter boys; and was very well qualified for his role as war artist; his pictures of the pilots of Fighter Command are proof of that. Therefore the artist of the haunted painting is one of the best … no, the best, for he understood the men that he immortalized.

So, no clue from the artist of the painting. Therefore it has to do with the Bader family and, my research has shown this might be so, and the ghostly face on the painting could be that of Douglas Bader's mother; and that would figure to be true when one looks at the image, which as stated, is always on the right-hand side of Douglas Bader's face. However, on further deeper research, I now categorically say that the 'image' on the paining, be that of some deity of Douglas Bader's past.

It is **not** his mother; who was a missionary in India. In 1938, Mr Plumb bought Bader's 1938 Ford car, as Bader was returning to his flying duties at that time; and from this line of investigation I know it is not Douglas Bader's mother. That I am certain.

RAF Cranwell play down that the painting of Douglas Bader is haunted. However, it has had an impact on someone at Cranwell, for I am reliably informed, that the painting was x-rayed to try and solve the mystery for it was said there was another painting underneath which, caused the image. But the x-ray showed no trace of any other painting underneath. The painting was then taken away to be chemically treated and, this proved very interesting; for when the Bader painting was being treated the ghostly image disappeared only to return again weeks after it was replaced back on the wall at RAF Cranwell. Apparently all tests for damp, mould, and ageing etcetera … have all proved negative.

So those are the facts … the painting of Group Captain Douglas Bader is haunted by a ghostly face

That is a fact, despite the denial by both the Ministry of Defence and RAF College Cranwell. The painting of Douglas Bader that hangs in the main dining room is haunted. The proof is in the photographs. And, with the haunted painting not readily available to the general public, I have shown here a set of 5 photographs, all taken from a different angle and position, plus a map to show the dining room.

All shown in **Ghost Stations™ 4** for the first time.

A HAUNTED HOLIDAY

The haunted Heathfield Cottage – Posing for their holiday snap are young Richard and Trevor

Many old wartime airfields have been given a new lease of life . . . some of the lucky ones being used by flying clubs, thus able to continue in a flying role.

Others were turned into a variety of uses, which include uses in the leisure industry.

The Domestic Site of the old Royal Naval Air Station St. Merryn - HMS Vulture - has been converted into a holiday camp.

One day a cleaning lady was working in one of the huts on the old airfield, when suddenly, she 'felt' a presence, and an urge to look around at the bed, which was just behind her.

She turned to see a pilot sitting on the bed. He was wearing a fur-lined, leather jacket and similar style knee-length boots.

He had in his hand a leather-flying helmet. "I was petrified," said the cleaning lady and, she refused to work in that hut again.

From 1978 to 1980, Squadron Leader Colin Pomeroy served as a Flight Commander on No. 42 Squadron at RAF St. Mawgan, flying Nimrod aircraft, and as St Mawgan has only a few married quarters located within its confines, he lived in one of five ex-Royal Navy Officers quarters at the old RNAS St. Merryn.

During this period he became very friendly with the members of the Padstow/Trevose Head Lifeboat crew, and on one of his visits, the conversation turned to RNAS St. Merryn and the haunted holiday hut.

"One couldn't hope to meet a more 'down- to-earth' and level headed lady than the one to whom I was talking," he said.

"She was quite emphatic that there was one of the huts on the old airfield into which she would no longer enter."

And Squadron Leader Pomeroy added: "I cannot, obviously, vouch for the accuracy of her story; I can, though, vouch for the sincere way in which it was told to me."

From a haunted holiday hut to a haunted holiday cottage and this one was so bad it made the Hodgkins family pack-up and leave . . . before their holiday had ended.

This haunted holiday cottage was one on what was part of the old Holmsley airfield in Hampshire.

The old airfield, known officially as Holmsley South, was not far from Christchurch and was very close to the New Forest.

During the war years it housed some Coastal Command Squadrons and some Canadian Fighter Squadrons before being taken over by the Americans to become Station No. 455. American B-26 Marauders then operated from the airfield that closed soon after the war ended.

It had a brief hectic life and after the war the Forestry Commission quickly reclaimed the bulk of the airfield. One section is now used as a public road and, some of the buildings at the edge of the airfield in the Forest Road area were turned into self-catering holiday cottages.

One of those holiday cottages was called 'Heathfield Cottage' in Forest Road, Holmsley, on the very edge of the wartime airfield. The cottage was isolated and the remains of the wartime runway were only a few hundred yards away.

In the summer of 1972, Mr. and Mrs. Hodgkins and their two children decided to again spend a holiday at 'Heathfield Cottage' but this time, Mrs. Hodgkins took her parents along.

"My husband, myself and our two young sons had for a couple of years spent a self-catering holiday at Heathfield Cottage in Hampshire. We loved every minute of our holiday and nothing unusual happened," said Mrs. Eileen Hodgkins.

But, their third holiday at the cottage was to be very different as she explains: "Something happened on that third holiday that has made a lasting impression on me and is as vivid today as it was then."

But what was that?

Had the Hodgkins family unlocked the Time Zone?

It started the day they arrived at the cottage - Eileen Hodgkin's mother said she was horrified by the feeling she experienced on entering the cottage, but she said nothing at the time, so as not to upset the holiday.

"Unbeknown also to any of us was the fact that my mother was sleeping on a bed previously unused by any of us," said Eileen

"This turned out to be not a proper single bed but an old fashioned laying out board. This was not discovered until the next day," she added.

It started on their very first night, and repeated every night the same pattern.

But, for Eileen and her husband, they were unaware of what was going on each night . . . they just knew it did not feel right but, thought no more about it - for they were on holiday - as Eileen explains:

"My husband and I were both awakened during the night by heavy footsteps going down the stairs, doors opening and closing, chairs being scraped on the kitchen floor and the sound of china and cutlery.

"I am afraid my husband's reaction was 'Can't your parents go through the night without having to make a cup of tea and wake everybody up . . . tell them we are on holiday and to enjoy themselves.'"

The next day Eileen found that her parents did not bring up the subject so she thought it better not to say anything.

She still decided to stay silent even though the same thing happened night after night, much to the annoyance of Eileen and her husband.

After a few days, Richard, who was 8 years old, the eldest of the two boys, started talking about the nice man in a leather jacket and goggles and he said to his mother:

"The nice man mummy who comes and stands by my bed and 'Smiles at me'."

It was only then that Eileen and her husband realised that there was some presence in the cottage - but, not harmful in any way.

"Richard was not in the least distressed by the visits from the nice man in the leather jacket," said Eileen.

"But, it did make us wonder what was going on. After a few days my parents wanted to know why it was we could not sleep at night and had to keep getting up and making tea, disturbing them both. It was only then did we realise that all four of us were hearing exactly the same thing."

And Eileen Hodgkins added: "My mother and I are both inclined to be fey but, I can assure you that both my father and husband are the most down to earth men you could meet and, before this, the pair of them would have scoffed at any suggestion of ghosts! - I don't know about my father but it shook my husband."

The children took it all as part of the holiday and could not understand what all the fuss was about - to them it was a great adventure. But for their parents and grand-parents it was a nerve shattering experience and very upsetting.

"The feeling in the cottage was one of despair and sadness," said Eileen Hodgkins, "the only room you did not experience this was in the bathroom."

The Hodgkins family were so distressed with it all; they cut short their holiday and returned home … it was just too much for them.

It is difficult to say why it happened and I can only suggest that they bordered on the edge of the Time Zone, but did not have the psychic power to enter.

It is known that the only room, in which they did not have a feeling of sadness, was the bathroom.

This room had been built on after the war and was not part of the original cottage.

The cottage was on the very edge of the old wartime airfield and during the war it was used as a billet for the officers. So, it had very strong wartime connections, which could well explain the apparition that visited young Richard's room.

Royal Air Force, Canadian and American were stationed at Holmsley South airfield during those hectic war years. For many it was their last place on earth.

The Hodgkins family had been twice before to Heathfield Cottage for a holiday and, had enjoyed themselves very much. They had not felt or heard anything unusual during their previous holidays at the cottage. But, with hindsight, Mrs. Eileen Hodgkins did say:

"We remember hearing what we took at the time to be a number of birds in the roof space . . . making a great deal of noise . . . that is probably all it was but one can't help wondering after our third visit."

The Haunted Holiday is a mystery and, it would be interesting to know if anyone else had experienced anything paranormal in Heathfield Cottage, before or since, the Hodgkins experience - for as Mrs. Eileen Hodgkins says:

"Believe me, it is something none of us in the family will forget."

THE HAUNTED SQUADRON

In April 1931 No 40 Squadron was reformed as a bomber squadron at Upper Heyford … the squadron badge being a broom and, it was not long before it became known as the haunted squadron with the broom taking on a more sinister meaning.

During the First World War No 40 Squadron had served on the Western Front as a Fighter Squadron. It disbanded in 1919.

On 26 September 1933, No 40 Bomber Squadron was returning to its home base at RAF Abingdon in Berkshire after exercises in Scotland. During these exercises the squadron had used the old Royal Flying Club aerodrome at Montrose. No 40 Bomber Squadron was the first Service Squadron to use the airfield as a base since the eerie disaster that depleted No 2 Squadron in 1914.

As No 40 Bomber Squadron flew southwards that September morning in 1933 a strange supernatural event began to unfold ... almost a re-run of No 2 Squadrons disaster who, had returned at the same time ... Flight Sergeant Christian and his passenger in Fairey Gordon K1732 encountered thick mist over Northumberland and disappeared.

The earlier incident was in 1914. No 2 Squadron left Montrose and headed south for Netheravon on Salisbury Plain on 15 May 1914. They were to take part in exercises but over Yorkshire they flew into thick ground mist. Lieutenant John Empson and A. G.

Cudmore in a B. E. 2A, No 331, attempted to land at Hutton Bonville near Northallerton. The aircraft went through a hedge and overturned, killing Empson and Cudmore in the process.

After an almost identical disaster with No 40 Bomber Squadron many high ranking people linked the accident to the supernatural influence associated with the old aerodrome at Montrose.

Still fresh in the minds of many Service Personnel being the Ghost of Montrose Aerodrome; but the 40 Squadron incident was much more mysterious.

A day after aircraft Fairey Gordon K1732 disappeared, an aircraft wheel was washed up on the East Coast and Christian's body floated in three days later. The body of his passenger was never found.

And stranger still... aircraft K1732 was never on charge to Number 40 Squadron. It was struck off charge on ... 26 September 1933. The very day this aircraft is said to have crashed.

How very, very strange; which proves that facts are stranger than fiction.

IS THERE A PARALLEL DIMENSION?

Stranger than Fiction. Let me tell you a story which might give you much more than food for thought but, leave you in no doubt that there is a parallel dimension. In March 1975 Dick 'Dickie' Smith was setting out for Ostend in his light aircraft and. was just near Chelmsford when he picked up a faint message ... he could not believe it. As a former wartime bomber pilot, Dickie knew it was an S.O.S. from a crew about to ditch.

The message was very faint but Dickie was able to establish it was from Halifax LL413 and sounded like May Day for aircraft going down. "I tried to trace the message but it only got fainter, then suddenly it was gone," said Dickie.

So what was the ghostly message? I researched and found that a four-engined Halifax bomber, number LL413, from No 297 Squadron did in fact fail-to-return from an air sea rescue search over the North Sea on 3 March 1945. It just vanished without trace.

But how could Dickie Smith pick up a message three decades later? That, for me, proves that there is a parallel dimension or as I have put it, a Time Zone, for it was clearly the last message he heard from the aircraft. From what I could find out it just disappeared in 1945 and was never found.

Then three decades later more proof to back my Time Zone theory, for that is not the first time such messages from the past have been received. Alan Holmes, a radio officer on the QE2, said he received a message from the liner, Queen Mary.

Nothing strange about that, you might say. But it was strange - very strange for at the time he received the message the Queen Mary was no longer in service as a liner. She had been turned into a conference centre at Long Beach harbour in California.

Could it have been a hoax? Not possible. The message was in a code procedure, which was no longer used. Holmes recognized it immediately as a routine position check being transmitted from the Queen Mary liner to Portishead Radio at Burnham in Somerset. So that does prove the BBH Time Zone theory.

The answer that Alan Holmes gave might also explain the ghostly message that Dickie Smith received. He said, "The signal had bounced out into space and just zipped around until it found its way back to earth."

A very logical answer; but no one can come up with a better explanation than my BBH Time Zone theory. A Parallel Dimension and Time Zone are one and the same.

Radio is a very new invention and the messages are still winging their way through space. Then, out there in space … they might be received and inform those receiving it that there is life on another planet.

Remember, one light-year is about ten million, million kilometres. And to give you an example, the star Vega, is a mere twenty-six light-years away from the sun. Vega is one of the three bright stars that dominate the western sky during the early winter months. It can be seen very clearly in the early evening.

Light travels, sound travels, so why not feelings and emotions? There is much that we still do not understand, despite our so-called advancement of technology.

www.ghoststations.com

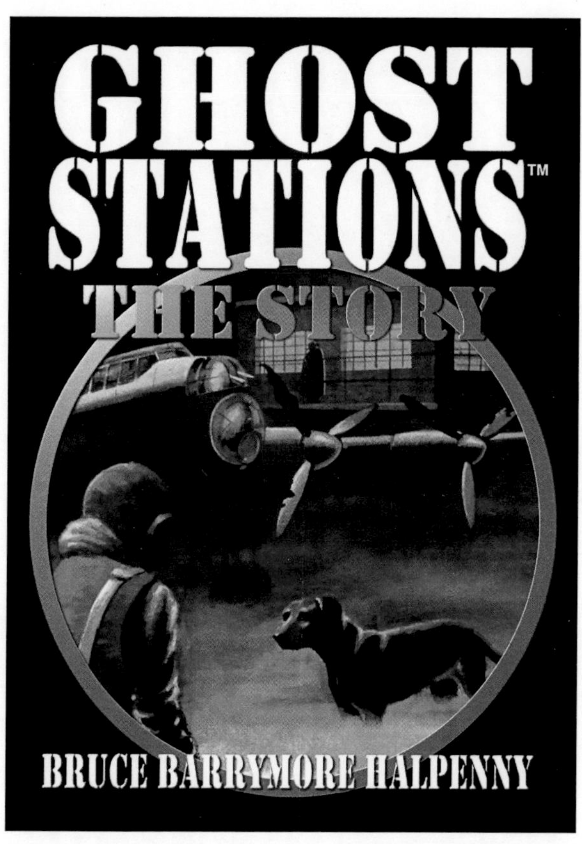

The Story about, GHOST STATIONS™, featuring special stories, photographs and a glossary of the abbreviations used in the GHOST STATIONS™ Series.
GHOST STATIONS™ The Story is a companion to the Series of GHOST STATIONS™ Books.

www.ghoststations.com

THE NEW GHOST STATIONS™

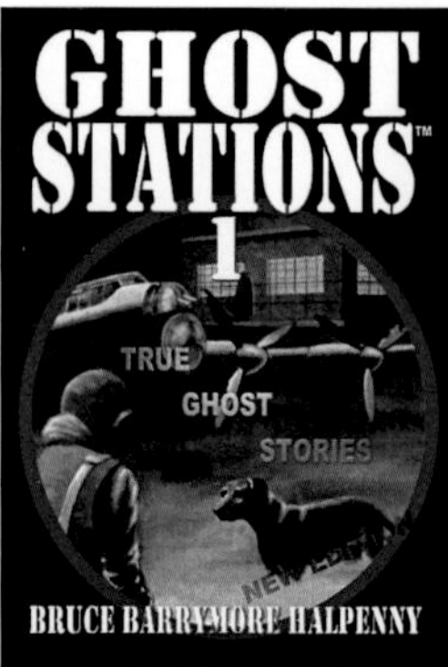

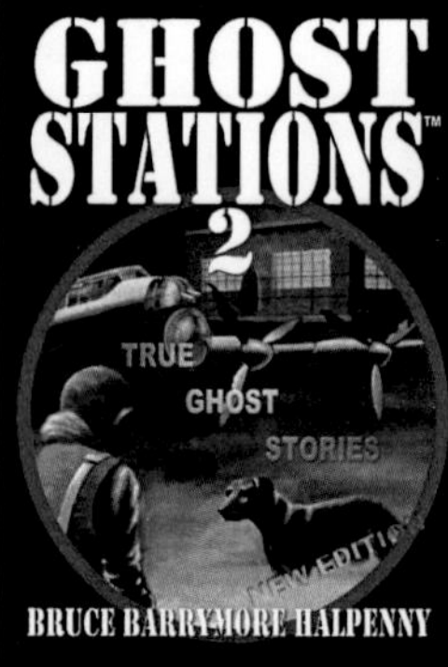

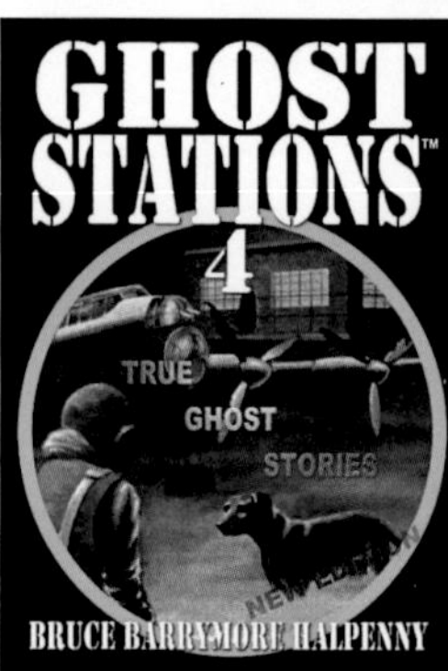

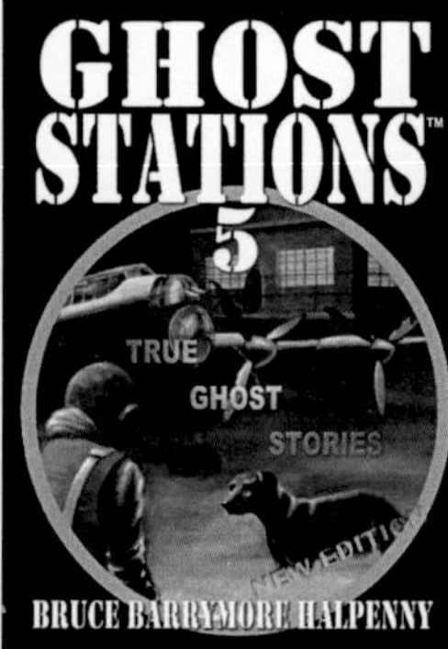

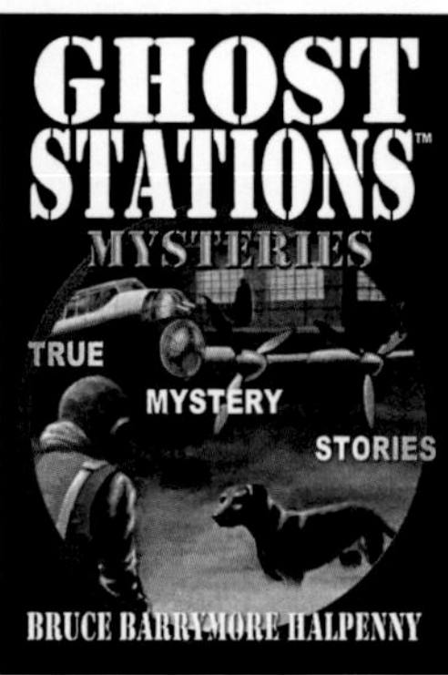

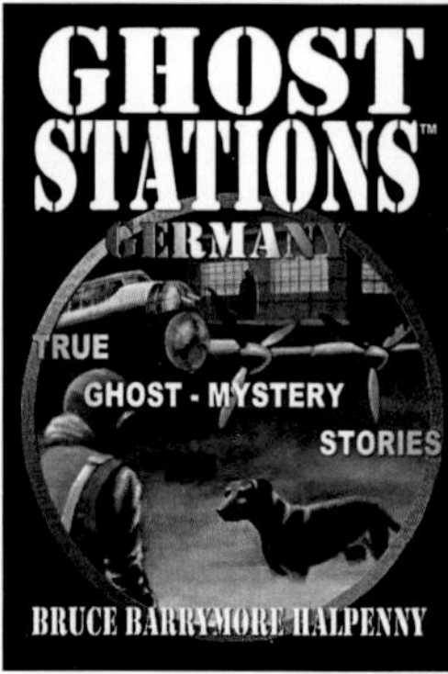

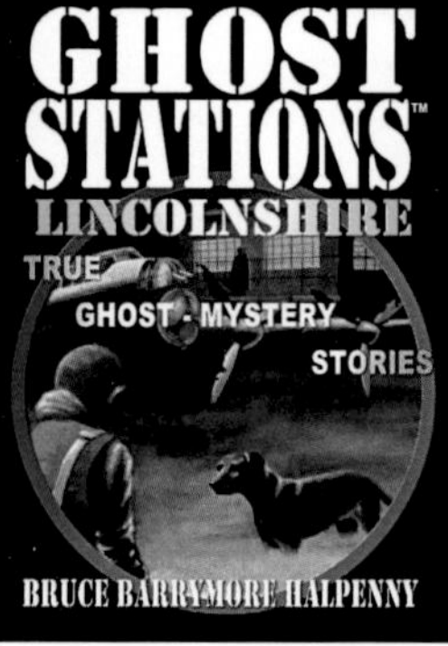

… And more to follow!!!